Cleopatra's Egypt

Cleopatra's Egypt

BY JEAN DAVIS

PUBLISHERS   Grosset & Dunlap   NEW YORK

An imaginary portrait of Cleopatra painted by an unknown artist some time after her death.

Foreword

In Africa, more than five thousand years ago, on the banks of the river Nile, a civilization began to grow and flourish in the land we call Egypt. This civilization is probably one of the oldest of all. At a time when men in Europe were little better than savages, the Egyptian people, ruled by Egyptian pharaohs, were living peacefully in villages, towns, and cities. They had developed a calendar and a written language. They had learned to irrigate their fields, were building temples for their gods and tombs for themselves, and were creating beautiful things.

For centuries the country, hemmed in on both the east and west by deserts, prospered in peace. Then invaders from Asia called the Hyksos, pushed into Egypt, bringing horses, which were unknown to the Egyptian people, and war chariots. They conquered Egypt and ruled it for one hundred and fifty years, until courageous Egyptian leaders raised an army and drove them out.

By this time the Egyptians had become a military nation and had developed a great interest in the countries lying to the northeast. Soon Egyptian pharaohs were leading armies into Syria, conquering one king after another, exacting tribute from them, and building Egypt into the most powerful empire in the world. Trade with other countries flourished, and Egypt enjoyed many years of peace and prosperity.

At last a pharaoh came to the throne who was more interested in establishing a new religion than in holding the empire together. Realizing this, rebellious Syrian kings refused to pay their tribute and broke away from Egypt. Although some of their city-states were reconquered by later pharaohs, the Egyptian Empire never fully regained its strength, and the pharaohs themselves began to lose their hold over their own people. The priests of the Egyptian god, Amon, had become so wealthy, because of the tribute they exacted from the pharaohs and the people, that the high priest now had almost as much power as a king.

Meanwhile, foreigners had been moving into Egypt to join the army as paid soldiers, to find positions of importance for themselves in the royal court, or simply to settle with their families in the

Nile valley. Gradually, as the powers of the pharaohs diminished, foreigners even gained control of the throne of Egypt. Some of these foreign rulers were good, others were bad. One Persian king treated the Egyptians so terribly that when, in 332 B.C., Alexander the Great, the king of Macedon, whose father had conquered Greece, came marching into Egypt, the people welcomed him gladly.

Alexander drove out the Persians. Then he turned the Egyptian army and navy over to Greek officers, established a new city called Alexandria on the Nile Delta as the capital of Egypt, and left to carry on his wars elsewhere.

After Alexander's death, some years later, one of his most trusted generals, a Macedonian Greek named Ptolemy, managed to make himself the king of Egypt. This was the beginning of a line of kings, all Ptolemies. A few ruled well, but the others were a cruel lot of men who taxed the people heavily and spent much of the wealth of Egypt on luxurious living.

During the reigns of the Ptolemies, thousands of Greeks settled in colonies along the Nile, and many of them married Egyptians. Although the Greeks respected the antiquity and the religion of Egypt, they felt superior to the Egyptian people, learned little about them, and often could not speak or read their language. Since Greeks held all the positions of importance in the court and in the government, Egyptians who wanted to rise in the world frequently took Greek names and spoke Greek. And in 69 (or 68) B.C. when Cleopatra, daughter of Ptolemy XIII was born, Egypt, which was still the richest country in the world, was in some ways as Greek as it was Egyptian.

Contents

	FOREWORD	9
I.	A BAD BEGINNING	15
II.	A POWERFUL FRIEND	23
III.	UP THE NILE	33
IV.	END OF A DREAM	47
V.	A WISE AND GLAMOROUS QUEEN	55
VI.	FOR EGYPT AND CAESARION	61
VII.	TRIUMPH AND TROUBLE	69
VIII.	TERRIBLE DAYS	77
IX.	DEATH CHEATS OCTAVIAN	87

ACKNOWLEDGMENT

For their courtesy and cooperation in supplying the pictures on the pages indicated, the author gives grateful acknowledgment to the following:

Charles Phelps Cushing: Pages 20-21, 33, 37, 50-51, 52-53, 58-59, 60, 61, 69, 90-91, back endsheet.

Culver Pictures, Inc.: Pages 6, 9, 11, 14, 15, 16-17, 18, 22, 23, 25, 36, 38, 40-41, 47, 48, 55, 62, 84.

The Bettmann Archive: Front endsheet, page 44.

New York Public Library: Page 46, 63.

Professor Mariano Leone, of Naples, Italy, for paintings commissioned especially for this book. Pages 26-27, 28-29, 30, 31, 32, 34-35, 54, 65, 66-67, 68, 70, 72-73, 74-75, 76, 77, 78-79, 80, 82-83, 86, 87, 88-89, 92-93.

Cleopatra's
Egypt

Head from a statue of a woman resembling Cleopatra VII

Acquired in Italy

Limestone, c. 50–40 BC

BM GR 1879.7-12.15 (Sculpture 1873)

© 2001 The British Museum
Printed by Blue Cube Ltd, Denham, Uxbridge, UB9 5ED

ISBN 0-7141-4205-0

9 780714 142050

ISBN 0-7141-4203-4

9 780714 142036

The Emperor Augustus (27 BC–AD 14)
Roman sardonyx cameo
H. 12.8 cm
BM Cat. of Engraved Gems 3577

© 2001 The British Museum
Printed by Blue Cube Ltd. Denham, Uxbridge, UB9 5ED

I. A Bad Beginning

Cleopatra was born in the royal palace in Alexandria, in the Nile Delta, some time during the winter of 69-68 B.C. History does not record the exact date of her birth, nor even the name of her mother. Her father was Ptolemy XIII, a Macedonian Greek, who was king of all Egypt.

The Egyptian people as a whole thought of Ptolemy as their pharaoh and gave him the titles which had been bestowed on all their pharaohs, such as "Child of the Sun," and "Chosen of Amon." But in Alexandria, Ptolemy XIII was called Auletes, meaning "the Piper," because of his habit of playing the flute when he should have been attending to the affairs of the country. The Egyptians pictured him on the walls of their temples as wearing the stiff linen kilt and the tall double crown worn by the ancient pharaohs. But, except for the fact that Auletes' robe was usually purple and richly embroidered, he dressed like any other Greek. Although Auletes ruled Egypt, he probably had seen little of it beyond the walled city of Alexandria, and he did not even speak Egyptian. He spoke Greek.

Little Cleopatra, growing up in the luxurious palace in Alexandria, running through the marble halls with their slender Grecian columns, and playing in the beautiful palace gardens, spoke Greek, too. We know nothing of her childhood,

but surely she must have spent some time with her younger sister, Arsinoe, although she disliked her, and with her two small brothers who were called Ptolemy XIV and Ptolemy XV. And it may be that the royal tutors with whom her elder half-sister, Berenice, studied, were her tutors also.

Cleopatra must have been a good student, for she learned to speak several languages, including Egyptian. If she had questions which her tutors could not answer, she could send for one of the

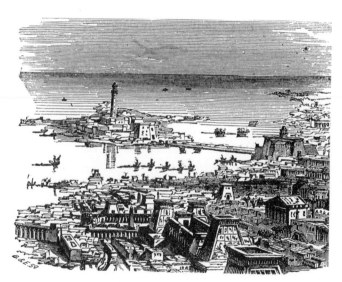

Part of Alexandria showing the palace at the end of the embankment which connected Pharos Lighthouse with the mainland.

Pharos Lighthouse at the entrance of the harbor of Alexandria. Metal mirrors in the cupola reflected light from a wood fire so that it could be seen 34 miles away.

professors from the museum (which was really a kind of university), near the palace, or procure rolled papyrus books from the huge library which housed the largest collection of books in the world.

Some of those books undoubtedly told her something about the Egyptian people whom she hoped one day to rule. But the Egyptians themselves knew little or nothing about Cleopatra, their pretty Greek princess who was growing up in Alexandria. Indeed, to most of the dwellers along the Nile, their capital city seemed so far away that they hardly thought of it as a part of Egypt.

This beautiful city on the shore of the Mediterranean was a place of wide colonnaded avenues and blossoming trees. The magnificent palace, the temples, the public buildings, the monuments, and statues were made of white marble which gleamed in the sun. The flower gardens, fragrant and bright with color, bloomed the year long.

People of many nationalities thronged the streets on foot, on horseback, in litters, or in chariots. Greeks, Persians, Romans, Syrians, Jews, black-skinned Nubians, men from far-off India, and Egyptians, all went about their own affairs, speaking their own languages and wearing what they would have worn in their own countries.

The city quays were noisy and busy, and the harbor was filled with ships from foreign lands. At the entrance to the harbor stood the great Pharos Lighthouse, built of white marble and more than five hundred feet high, from which, we are told, a light could be seen thirty-four miles out at sea, and which was one of the Seven Wonders of the World.

But of all this wealth and splendor in Alexandria, the dwellers along the Nile knew little. Whether they lived in mud-hut villages or in towns and cities, many of them worked as Egyptians before them had worked for nearly three thousand years. Farmers, wearing the Greek tunic instead of the ancient Egyptian loin cloth or kilt, plowed and planted their fields with the help of their oxen, and harvested their crops. Shaven-headed priests carried on services and made sacrifices in the temples of Egyptian gods. Scribes with their palettes, ink pots, and brushes wrote letters on pieces of papyrus for those who could not write. They also kept track of tribute paid to the priests and taxes collected by representatives of the king. They tallied cargoes, which were loaded aboard or unloaded from freight boats on the Nile, and kept

accounts for wealthy Egyptians or Greeks who lived on large estates.

Boys went to school. Girls learned to spin and weave, though Egyptian cotton was now beginning to take the place of the fine linen for which Egypt had once been so famous. Merchants offered their wares in the market places, taking their payment in Greek coins instead of the old Egyptian copper utens. Artists, sculptors, potters, goldsmiths, leather-tanners, glass-blowers, carpenters, and other craftsmen usually labored from daylight till dark. And everyone, rich or poor, was dependent, as Egyptians always had been, on the rising and falling of the Nile.

This great river, which flows north for more than three thousand miles to the Mediterranean Sea, has three sources in the lakes and highlands of the eastern part of Africa. Every year melting snows and spring rains at these sources cause the Nile to swell until it overflows its banks and inundates the land. When the water begins to recede, it leaves behind a layer of rich black earth so

The Nile recedes, leaving rich black earth.

fertile that Egyptian farmers can often grow three crops a year. In Cleopatra's time a "good Nile" meant, as it had meant for centuries, a good year for Egypt. A "poor Nile" sometimes meant starvation.

Since the Egyptians did not know the sources of the Nile, they believed that the rising and falling of the river were caused by their god, Osiris. This belief and the welfare of the Egyptian people did not interest their pharaoh, Ptolemy XIII. Cleopatra's father cared nothing for what his subjects were thinking or doing as long as they paid their taxes and produced wealth for him to spend.

Ever since the days of Ptolemy I, all kings had regarded Egypt as one vast estate belonging to whatever pharaoh happened to be ruling. They owned the entire land and rented it out to their people. They or their officials determined for the people what crops should be planted, what animals should be raised, what articles should be manufactured, what should be exported, and what taxes should be collected. Yet, in spite of this, most of the Ptolemies had little interest in the welfare of their people. When, during the reign of Ptolemy XIII, there was a "poor Nile" for two years in succession and many Egyptians were hungry, Auletes did not care at all. Living luxuriously in his palace, Cleopatra's father drank heavily, gave wild parties, played the flute, and worried, with good reason, about holding his throne.

On the other side of the blue Mediterranean Sea lay Rome, and Rome was casting envious eyes at Egypt. By conquering or annexing all the lands bordering on the Mediterranean, including Syria, which had once been part of the Egyptian Empire, the Roman Republic had become the strongest nation on the earth. Now all signs indicated that Rome was planning to take over Egypt which, although second to Rome in power, was still the richest country in the world. And if Egypt were conquered and annexed by Rome, what would happen to Auletes?

Gathering together all the money he could lay his hands on, this flute-playing pharaoh, during the year that his daughter Cleopatra was ten, sailed to Rome, hoping to bribe the Roman Senators and their Consul, the mighty Julius Caesar, to let him rule Egypt in peace. But while he was gone, the Alexandrians began to feel the effects of the famine caused by two years of a "poor Nile." Many were hungry, and many more were angry because Auletes, in spite of taxing them severely, had done nothing to keep the irrigation canals in good repair or to build up the defenses of the country. When he returned to Alexandria more than a year later, after having gained the support of the Romans through bribery, his own

Ptolemy XIII, father of Cleopatra.

people turned against him and drove him out of Egypt.

Once more Auletes went to Rome and then to Syria, where he stayed for three years. During this time his daughter Berenice seized the throne and, with a husband chosen for her by the Alexandrians, she ruled the country well. This made Auletes furious. By offering huge bribes to the Governor of Syria, he persuaded him to send an army of Roman infantry and cavalry against Berenice. The cavalry, commanded by a young Roman named Mark Antony, captured the Egyptian port and fortress of Pelusium, which guarded the border between Syria and Egypt. Then, with the infantry, they pushed on toward Alexandria, burst open the city gates, and invaded the streets.

Fourteen-year-old Cleopatra, watching from the palace windows, heard the clanking of Roman arms and the cries of the terrified Alexandrians. Berenice's husband was killed in the fighting and later, when Auletes had returned to rule Egypt, Berenice herself was put to death at her father's command. Roman cavalry and infantry were left in the city to keep order, and there was peace in Alexandria for almost four years.

Meanwhile Cleopatra grew from a pretty, mischievous, high-spirited girl into a courageous, intelligent, charming young woman. She was still mischievous and high-spirited, but she could also be very dignified whenever it seemed necessary.

What did she look like? No one really knows. We read in books written soon after her lifetime that there was "a sweetness in the sound of her voice," and that she was graceful and quick in her movements. We see from the coins which bear her profile and from a bust in the British Museum that her features were beautiful. But no record has ever been found which tells us of the color of her skin, her hair, or her eyes.

She was an ambitious young woman, and since she was now the eldest child in the royal family, she thought, of course, that when her father died she would become the sole ruler of Egypt. But Auletes had other plans. When, in the words of the ancient Egyptians, he "walked down the Western Horizon," during the year 55 B.C., he left a will which shocked and dismayed his daughter.

In his will he decreed that Cleopatra, who was then about seventeen, should marry Ptolemy XIV, her ten-year-old brother, and that they should rule Egypt together. He also decreed that the young king and queen were to be placed under the guardianship of the Roman people.

Marriages between brothers and sisters were not unusual in the royal families of Egypt, but Ptolemy XIV was far too young to be a husband to Cleopatra. He was also too young to realize that the three men who had been appointed to advise him were cruel, scheming scoundrels. Their names were Potheinos, Theodotus, and Achillas. All three had one aim — to get rid of Cleopatra so that young Ptolemy would become the only ruler of Egypt. Then, through their influence over him, they could gain the power they craved.

How it happened no one will ever know, for we have no records to tell us, but, after two years or so, these men seemed to have caused a terrible quarrel between Cleopatra and her brother. Cleopatra was forced to leave the palace and flee to Syria with a few loyal followers.

She was only nineteen or twenty years old and certainly not accustomed to the hardships of army life. Yet she set up headquarters in the desert and sent messengers throughout Syria with the word that she needed troops who would help her fight her way back into Egypt, and would pay them well.

It was a strange conglomeration of men who answered her call. Bandits who had nothing better to do, bearded desert tribesmen with bows and lances, runaway slaves, and rough Roman soldiers who had deserted their own leaders gathered at her camp. When all was ready they loaded their camels and oxcarts with supplies and marched toward Pelusium, where young Ptolemy was strongly established with his three advisers and a large army, all determined to keep Cleopatra out of Egypt.

Setting up her camp on the sandy coast of the Mediterranean, a few miles west of Pelusium, Cleopatra with her army prepared to attack her brother's forces. But before that attack could begin, spies and messengers brought alarming news to both camps.

For some time the Romans had been engaged in a civil war as two great generals, Gnaeus Pompey and Julius Caesar, fought one another for the right to control the Roman Republic. Now Pompey's army had been badly defeated in a battle on the plains of Pharsalia in Greece. Pompey had escaped with some of his men and, because he had once been very kind to Auletes, he was sailing toward Pelusium to seek help from Auletes' son, young King Ptolemy. Julius Caesar, with warships and soldiers, was in hot pursuit.

Hastily, Potheinos, Theodotus, and Achillas — the advisers of young Ptolemy — held a conference to decide what to do. Since Caesar was the victor and Pompey the loser at Pharsalia, there was little doubt in their minds what action to take. When Pompey's war galley dropped anchor at sea a short distance from Pelusium, Achillas, with several slaves and two Roman officers who were serving in the Egyptian army, sailed out in a small boat to meet him.

As the smaller vessel came alongside the galley, Achillas called out to Pompey, warning him that his warship could not come any farther into the harbor because of shallow water, and inviting him to come ashore in the Egyptian boat. Reluctantly,

An old print showing one artist's idea of how Julius Caesar

Pompey agreed to do so. With Pompey aboard, Achillas and his little company set out for shore. As their boat nosed up on the sand, Pompey rose to disembark. Immediately one of the Roman officers stabbed him in the back with his sword. Achillas and the other Roman officer then attacked him, killed him swiftly, and cut off his head.

A report of this villainous murder was quickly

landed at Alexandria. The Alexandrians, however, were not drawn up in battle lines to meet him.

carried to Cleopatra by one of her spies. Three days later she received another report which was even more disturbing. Julius Caesar had not continued in his pursuit of Pompey. Instead he had taken his warships and soldiers directly to Alexandria. Although a mob of angry Alexandrians had tried to prevent it, he had taken possession of the palace and installed his soldiers in the royal barracks. Now, as chief representative of the Roman people who had been appointed by Auletes to be the guardians of his children, Caesar demanded that Ptolemy XIV and his sister come at once to the palace, where he would help them settle their differences. Ptolemy XIV obeyed promptly. Cleopatra did not.

A device for raising water from the Nile to fill canals and irrigation ditches.

II. A Powerful Friend

What did the result of all this quarreling between their king and queen mean to the people dwelling along the Nile? Nothing as yet. Weeks would pass before the news could filter through the country that the pharaoh's palace in Alexandria had been taken over by a Roman general. And even when they heard it, most Egyptians would not be greatly excited.

It was at the time of the year when the Nile was high. Farmers with wooden plows were turning over the wet black earth wherever the waters had receded, and planting corn, most of which would be stored in the royal warehouses and temple granaries, or sent abroad. Ships, propelled by rowers when no strong wind filled the sails, were traveling up and down the river carrying passengers or freight. Cargo ships going north were loaded with wine, linen, cotton cloth, oil, papyrus, furniture, and glassware, produced in small factories owned by the ruling Ptolemies. Ships sailing south often carried timber, which was very scarce in Egypt and which was imported from other countries.

Merchants with camel caravans struggled across the eastern desert from the Red Sea to the Nile, bringing spices and rich textiles from India, as well as frankincense and myrrh which would be made up into perfumes and ointments for the royal court or for other wealthy Greeks. Shepherds, swineherds, raisers of cattle and horses, all watched over their beasts. In the temples, priests prepared animals for sacrifice as usual and worshipped the old Egyptian gods, while children from one end of the country to the other still listened to the stories of those gods.

Amun was the most powerful god, those children were told, but the best-loved god was Osiris. Once long, long ago, Osiris had been an Egyptian king and with his wife Isis, he had ruled the land wisely and well. Then his evil brother, Set, had killed him, buried his head in the ancient city of Abydos, and scattered pieces of his body in vari-

OSIRIS.

A statue of the god Osiris who ruled the dead.

ous parts of Egypt. Isis, his faithful wife, had found the pieces, put them with the head, and with the help of the jackal-headed god, Anubis, had brought Osiris back to life. Since Osiris was no longer able, however, to rule on earth, he became the beloved ruler and judge of the dead.

There were many other gods worshipped by the Egyptians, who believed also that their royal rulers were children of the gods and not of mortal men. Therefore, the rulers were divine, and Cleopatra, as Egypt's queen, was often called a divinity.

One wonders if she could have felt like a divinity as she paced back and forth in her tent near Pelusium or lay among her pillows there, trying to make up her mind what to do about Caesar's order to come to the palace. She dared not disobey him and did not want to, for she needed the friendship of this powerful general. But she was afraid that if she went to the palace, her brother and his advisers might have her killed before she reached Caesar, and she was also anxious to see the great man alone. She must have laughed aloud when she thought of the solution to her problem.

Boarding one of her ships, which was anchored near Pelusium, she sailed toward Alexandria, but before she reached the city she left the ship and stepped into a small boat with only one companion, her faithful servant and friend, Apollodorus. Dusk had fallen when they entered Great Harbor, where Caesar's ships were anchored outside the palace. Taking care not to attract the attention of the harbor guards, Apollodorus, a strong, tall Sicilian, made the little boat fast to one of the palace quays, while Cleopatra crouched in the bottom of the boat, keeping well out of sight.

As soon as it was dark, she stood up. Quickly Apollodorus wrapped her in a carpet which had been brought for the purpose, tied his bundle with a rope, hoisted it over his shoulder, and strode through the gate to the palace. Surely he was challenged by the sentries, and he probably told them that he was carrying a present to Caesar. At any rate, he gained the doorway of the luxuriously furnished room where the Roman leader was sitting, walked in, and laid down his bundle. As soon as the bundle was untied, the warm, disheveled, beautiful little queen rose to her feet, delighted because her trick had worked and curious about the great general who had taken over her palace.

As for Caesar, when he recovered from his surprise, he was filled with admiration for the plucky young girl who stood before him. Being a courteous gentleman, he probably ordered servants to bring her the finest food and wine in the palace, and for hours that night they talked together of many things.

Cleopatra explained to Caesar about her troubles with her brother, the king. Caesar, in turn, must have told her that Ptolemy's adviser, Potheinos, had refused to obey Caesar's command to disband the Egyptian army. Now, although Caesar would not allow King Ptolemy or Potheinos to leave the palace, twenty thousand of Ptolemy's soldiers were encamped nearby, ready to fight Caesar's four thousand troops, if ordered to do so. Caesar, whose soldiers occupied the palace and royal barracks, had sent hurriedly to Syria for reinforcements.

In addition to giving Cleopatra the news about the military situation, Caesar probably told her all about his life and conquests. He was charmed by her grace, her beauty, and her sweet voice. Before they parted, he was beginning to fall in love with her. Cleopatra, too, was falling in love, for although Caesar was thirty-four years older than she, he was keen, handsome, clever, courageous, and experienced in the ways of the world.

Cleopatra stands up before Julius Caesar.

To add to their pleasure in being together, each saw in the other a means of fulfilling an ambition. Caesar hoped that through Cleopatra he might gain control of some of the wealth of Egypt. Cleopatra realized that through Caesar, who was now the dictator of the most powerful country in the world, she might regain her throne.

She was overjoyed, therefore, when Caesar sent for young Ptolemy next morning and scolded him soundly for disobeying his father, who had decreed that Cleopatra and he should rule Egypt together. Caesar insisted that Cleopatra's throne should be restored to her and that Ptolemy should make peace with her immediately.

Poor Ptolemy! It was a shock to discover that Cleopatra was in the palace at all. To find that she and Caesar were already good friends was even worse. He ran out of the room in a temper, yanked off his golden diadem and dashed it to the floor, calling out to his friends and courtiers in the palace that he had been betrayed. The news spread like wildfire, and a crowd of furious Alexandrians who were loyal to young Ptolemy quickly surrounded the palace, ready to attack Caesar, crying out that he was a foreigner who had invaded their city and insulted their king.

Stepping boldly outside, in spite of jeers and threats, Caesar told the angry mob that he would soon hold a meeting at which everything would be explained. At that meeting he read aloud the will of Auletes and reminded everyone present, including Cleopatra and Ptolemy, that as a representative of the Roman people he had a right, according to Auletes' will, to settle the quarrel between the young rulers. Then he announced that Cleopatra would once more be the Queen of Egypt, and that he was giving the island of Cyprus to her sister, Princess Arsinoe, and to little Prince Ptolemy XV, to rule jointly.

By giving Cyprus, which had once belonged to

Caesar roundly scolds young Ptolemy for
in his will, and for trying to

disobeying his father's orders as expressed
rob Cleopatra of her throne.

Egypt, to the royal children, Caesar hoped to win the friendship of the Alexandrian people, and he might have done so if it had not been for Potheinos, who, in various ways, was constantly trying to stir up a revolt against Caesar among the Alexandrians.

One day Caesar heard from his barber that Potheinos and Achillas were plotting to murder him. Immediately, Caesar had Potheinos, who was still in the palace with Ptolemy, arrested and killed. Then, although his reinforcements from Syria had not yet arrived, he decided to burn the ships of the Egyptian fleet which were lying at anchor in the Great Harbor. When the ships were set ablaze, the leaping flames spread to buildings along the quay, including the famous library, which they completely destroyed. In the excitement and confusion that followed, sixteen-year-old Arsinoe, who was also a prisoner in the palace and who had never liked Cleopatra, managed to escape. With her tutor, she went to join the Egyptian army, which was still occupying part of the city.

Soon Caesar's spies reported to him that Arsinoe and the leaders of the Egyptian army were plotting to murder him and to rescue young King Ptolemy from the palace. Then they intended to overthrow Cleopatra so that Arsinoe could reign in her stead. This did not greatly disturb either Caesar or Cleopatra.

Caesar had already ordered fortifications built to protect his troops and the palace. Now he seized Pharos Lighthouse, which stood on the eastern tip of Pharos Island across from Alexandria at the main entrance to the harbor. A long mole or embankment connected the island with the city and separated this harbor into two bodies of water. One was Great Harbor. The other was called Harbor of Happy Return. The mole was called the Heptastadium.

CLEOPATRA'S EGYPT

From the palace windows, Cleopatra could see Great Harbor and the Heptastadium clearly, and there came a day when she must have watched the action on both with her fists clenched and her heart in her mouth. Caesar, whom she had grown to love dearly, was engaged in a battle with the Egyptian army on Pharos Island and in the harbor. He had led the Romans in a successful attack on the Egyptian forts and was crossing the Heptastadium with many of his men when suddenly he was trapped by the Egyptians, who closed in at both ends of the mole. Luckily, several boats belonging to the Roman fleet were nearby. Scrambling into them, the Romans rowed for all they were worth across Great Harbor. But the boat which Caesar had boarded was overloaded, and it capsized.

To Cleopatra's consternation, Caesar was forced to swim for his life. Ducking his head under the water to escape the arrows of the Egyptian archers, he dragged his crimson military cloak along by his teeth and held above the water several important documents which he had been carrying when disaster struck him. Before he was picked up by men in another of his boats, he had lost the cloak, which he prized highly because it was a sign of his rank, but the documents were safe. Jeering Alexandrians fished the cloak out of the water with a boat hook, and Caesar arrived at the palace wet, cold, and defeated.

More than four hundred of his men had been drowned, or killed by Egyptian arrows and spears, and he realized now that he had a real war on his hands. It was good news, therefore, when he learned that a large army of reinforcements from Syria was marching across the desert to bring him help. As he made plans for the days ahead, he decided to turn Ptolemy over to the Egyptian forces, who were still trying to rescue the boy from the palace. Then, if Ptolemy were killed in bat-

[28]

The battle in Great Harbor. The Heptastadium, not shown in the picture, was to the left.

tle, as Caesar felt sure he would be, Cleopatra could rule Egypt alone without breaking the terms of her father's will.

Sending for young Ptolemy, Caesar told him that he must go to the Egyptian headquarters to try to arrange some sort of peace terms for him. Ptolemy, who suspected at once why he was being sent out of the palace, tearfully begged to be allowed to remain, but to no avail. However, once he reached the Egyptian headquarters, Ptolemy proved that he was not the coward he seemed to be. At the head of the Egyptian army, he set out bravely to meet Caesar's reinforcements from Syria, who had already captured Pelusium and were marching south.

On hearing this, Caesar moved quickly and cleverly. In the dead of night, with not a light

The battle ends for young King Ptolemy, who is drowned when he falls into the Nile.

showing on any ship, he sailed with his men and his horses to a deserted place on the coast west of Alexandria. Then he marched swiftly south to join the Syrian reinforcements a few miles below Memphis on the west bank of the Nile. Together the two armies attacked young Ptolemy and his Egyptian forces.

Long-legged, pink flamingos and long-billed pelicans searching the Nile for fish must have taken flight quickly when the fighting began. All day the soft air of early summer resounded with the clashing of arms, the hum of arrows, the shrill neighing of the frightened horses, and the piteous cries of the wounded. That night the soldiers rested under the velvety, star-studded Egyptian sky. At dawn they were at it again.

War is such a noisy business that probably the sounds of fighting were heard in Memphis, that old Egyptian city which, hundreds of years earlier, had been the capital of the most powerful nation on earth. Surely the anxious villagers, in their little mud huts along the banks of the Nile near Memphis, were worried about what would happen to them if the Egyptian army was defeated. Would the Roman conquerors march south with their leader and lay waste the country with its wide fields of grain, which was almost ready for harvesting? Would they tear down the Egyptian temples? Would they carry away the sons of Egyptian farmers to be slaves?

The Romans did none of those things. By the end of the second day of fighting, the Egyptian army had been scattered in flight. Poor young King Ptolemy had fallen into the Nile and been drowned, weighed down by his golden corselet. And Caesar, with his soldiers and his cavalry, was soon on his way back to Alexandria with another victory to his credit.

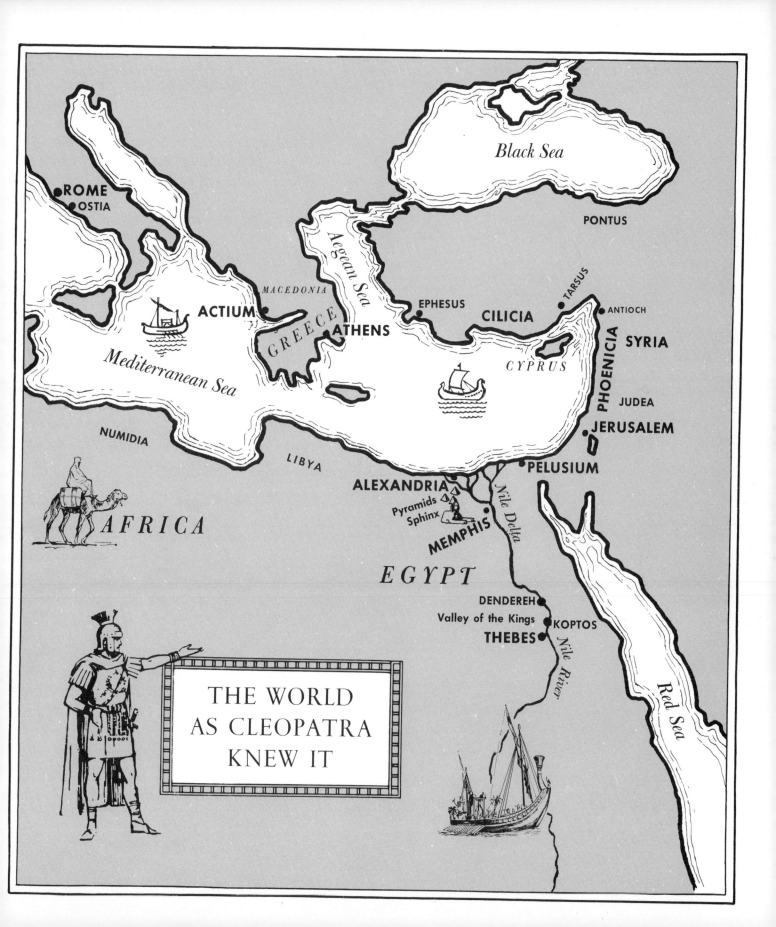

Black Sea

ROME
OSTIA

PONTUS

Aegean Sea

MACEDONIA

ACTIUM

GREECE

ATHENS

EPHESUS

TARSUS

CILICIA

ANTIOCH

SYRIA

CYPRUS

PHOENICIA

Mediterranean Sea

JUDEA

JERUSALEM

NUMIDIA

LIBYA

PELUSIUM

ALEXANDRIA

Pyramids
Sphinx

MEMPHIS

Nile Delta

AFRICA

EGYPT

DENDEREH

Valley of the Kings

KOPTOS

THEBES

Nile River

Red Sea

THE WORLD
AS CLEOPATRA
KNEW IT

Caesar, after his victory over the Egyptian army in the battle on the Nile, rides triumphantly into Alexandria at the head of his troops.

III. Up the Nile

Trumpets blared, lictors marched proudly with their fasces, standard-bearers held their silver eagles high, and banners floated in the breeze when Caesar and his cavalry soldiers rode triumphantly through the gates in the city wall of Alexandria. But there was no rejoicing among the citizens. Dressed in mourning, they gathered in the streets, watching the conqueror's troops go by, praying that he would be merciful to them, and holding before him statues of their gods to show him that they were ready to submit to his will.

Since parts of their beautiful city already had been destroyed by fire and fighting, Caesar decided, to their great relief, that they had been sufficiently punished for taking up arms against him. He was glad that the Alexandrian War was over and eager to return to his pleasant life in the palace. The rebellious Arsinoe had been arrested and sent to Rome, King Ptolemy XIV was dead, and peace had returned to Egypt.

Still acting as the Roman guardian of the royal children, Caesar soon announced that Cleopatra's youngest brother, to whom he had given the island of Cyprus, would now be known as King Ptolemy XV and would marry Cleopatra. The ten-year-old boy was, of course, a king and a husband in name only, and Cleopatra became for the first time the real ruler of Egypt. She also became Caesar's wife.

It did not matter to the Egyptians that Caesar already had a wife in Rome, because in Egypt a man could lawfully have more than one wife if he wished. And it pleased the people when they were told that the Roman dictator was descended from the gods, like their beautiful young queen. The marriage also removed from the minds of many of them any fear that Rome would invade, conquer, and annex Egypt.

As for Cleopatra, she had never been happier. She was deeply in love with Caesar and was as

Julius Caesar as a young man.

[33]

eager to show him the country over which she now ruled as he was to see it. Plans were soon in the making for a trip up the Nile, and when all was ready one spring day they set sail.

Caesar and Cleopatra traveled on the royal houseboat which was called a *thalamegos* by the Greeks. This magnificent ship, which was rowed by many oarsmen, was like a floating palace. It was several stories high, and the open decks were equipped with linen awnings cleverly arranged to shield the travelers at all hours of the day from the hot Egyptian sun. The colonnaded courts and the rooms were beautifully furnished in the Greek style, with the exception of the great dining hall, which was like the banqueting hall of an Egyptian pharaoh. There were shrines dedicated to Venus, the Roman goddess of love from whom Caesar claimed to be descended, and to the Greek god, Dionysus. There was even a small garden.

Aboard this beautiful ship, Caesar and Cleopatra, waited on by countless servants and entertained by dancers, actors, and musicians, sailed from Alexandria into the nearest branch of the Nile. Four hundred other ships followed them, carrying more servants and entertainers, stores of

Cleopatra and Julius Caesar travel

food and supplies, and several thousand soldiers. Whether Caesar took the soldiers along because he expected trouble from the Egyptians on the journey, or because he hoped to invade enemy country in the Sudan to the south, we do not know. At any rate, Caesar and those legionnaires must have had an interesting trip, and so must Cleopatra, who had seen little of her kingdom beyond the walls of Alexandria.

Sailing out of the branch of the Nile, the fleet emerged onto the river itself. It was not far to Memphis, and just north of that city the travelers stopped to see the three great Pyramids and the

Sphinx, which had stood in the desert on the west bank of the river for more than twenty-five hundred years. The Pyramids had been built by three pharaohs to be their tombs, or Houses of Eternity, for the ancient Egyptians believed that before a man died he must prepare a safe place where his body could lie unmolested and his spirit could live forever.

Looking at the Pyramids, Caesar must have wondered how men had ever been able to cut and raise the huge blocks of stone of which they were made, and then to fit them so closely together that not even a knife blade could be inserted be-

in the royal houseboat up the Nile.

The Great Sphinx and the Pyramids near Memphis. The face of the Sphinx was not so battered when Caesar saw it, and the casing of the Pyramids was probably still intact.

tween them. He must have wondered, also, about the Great Sphinx, that massive creature carved from rock, which has the body of a lion and the face of a man. The fact that these monuments were so old impressed the Roman general. He was interested, too, in the other monuments and temples which stood on both banks of the Nile.

Leaving the Pyramids, he sailed on with Cleopatra to Memphis, a few miles farther south. In this proud old city was a royal palace used by mighty pharaohs long ago, and more recently by some of the Ptolemies. Although there were people of several nationalities living in the city, it was still largely Egyptian in appearance and feeling.

Wherever Cleopatra appeared outside of Alexandria, her subjects fell prostrate before her as Egyptians had always fallen before their rulers. One can well imagine the excitement of the people in Memphis when she and Caesar visited the great temple there of the Egyptian god, Ptah. How they must have crowded the streets to see her! Black-haired, brown-skinned, dark-eyed people, lifting up their children to catch a glimpse of their beautiful queen and perhaps calling out to her the age-old greeting to all pharaohs, "Life! Prosperity! Health!"

When the fleet left Memphis little boys ran along the shore calling out questions to the Roman soldiers, who could not understand their language. And women, washing clothes at the edge of the Nile, stopped their work to stare in amazement at the royal yacht and the long line of ships which followed it.

From Memphis the royal party traveled on to the Fayum. This was a rich section of the country which had grown up around an oasis in the desert on the west bank of the Nile. Here, on the shores of Lake Moeris, which had been used by pharaohs and their families nearly twenty centuries earlier, wealthy Greek families had built their homes.

A view of Memphis on the east bank of the Nile as Caesar and Cleopatra may have seen it.

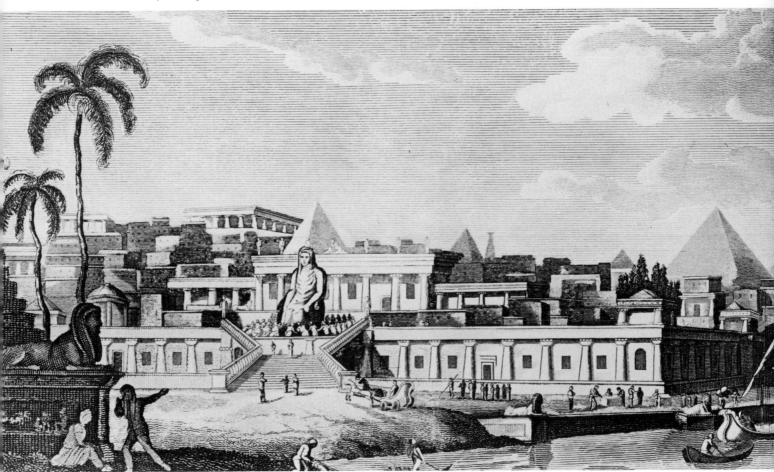

[37]

Here, too, in a prosperous town called Crocodilopolis was an ancient Egyptian temple to Sobk, the crocodile god, where priests tended a sacred crocodile which they had adorned with jewels, feeding it gently by hand every day. When the crocodile died of over-feeding or old age, its body would be carefully embalmed and placed in a holy vault. Then another sacred crocodile would be found to be worshipped in its place.

Animal worship of this kind had not always been the custom in Egypt. It is true that since the early days of Egyptian history, the Egyptians had worshipped gods which were pictured as having human bodies and the heads of animals or birds. They had also sometimes selected a single very special animal to provide a body through which a god might act. This animal was cared for and respected as were the god's statues, but it was not worshipped. Later, however, at about 1000 B.C., when Egypt was beset by troubles and invaded by foreigners, the custom of worshipping the animals themselves had sprung up among the Egyptian people. The Greeks were very scornful of this and so, probably, was Caesar. One can see him turning away from the crocodile to devote his attention to the elaborate system of canals, walls, and sluices by which the Egyptians had regulated the rise and fall of water into Lake Moeris seventeen hundred years earlier and which was still in use.

Leaving the Fayum, Caesar and Cleopatra sailed on with their fleet up the Nile, past towns and mud-hut villages set among palm trees, past more ancient temples and monuments, partly destroyed by war or by the passing of years, until they came at last to the ruins of the city of Akhetaton. Whether or not they stopped to view the ruins, we do not know. But it was an interesting city for it had been founded by a most unusual man named Akhenaton.

This young pharaoh, who came to the throne in 1375 B.C., had turned his back on all the gods his people worshipped. "There are not many gods," he told his subjects. "There is only *one* God, whom I call Aton. He created the earth and all the people on it, wherever they may live. We are all His children. Aton is the only God — the true God. All other gods are false."

This idea did not please the Egyptians. They refused to forsake their old gods, and in Thebes, which was then the capital, the priests of Amon were furious when workmen, sent by Akhenaton, removed Amon's name from statues, temples, and tombs. So strongly did the people and the priests oppose Akhenaton and his one God that at last the pharaoh built a new capital some distance north of Thebes. He named it Akhetaton and dedicated it to the worship of Aton.

It was a beautiful city of wide streets, spacious gardens, large estates, and good homes for even the poorest of the laborers. But when Akhenaton died, the city was quickly deserted. People had not been able to accept the new religion which he had tried to teach them. They hated him because he believed so firmly in the brotherhood of man that he would not go to war against Egypt's enemies, even to hold the Egyptian Empire together. And calling him "the criminal of Akhetaton," they went back to the worship of their old gods.

Akhetaton fell into ruins which are still there to remind the world that in ancient Egypt there lived the first man known to history who grasped the truth which most civilized men believe today — that there is only one God and that He is the Father of all mankind.

It is doubtful that Caesar and Cleopatra landed to look over the ruins of Akhetaton. They would have known little of the place or of the man who founded it. Only a few days' journey beyond it lay Ptolemais, a busy prosperous city settled by Greeks. Then came Abydos, that ancient city

Queen Nefertiti, the beautiful wife of the pharaoh, Akhenaton, supposed to be the first man who believed in one God.

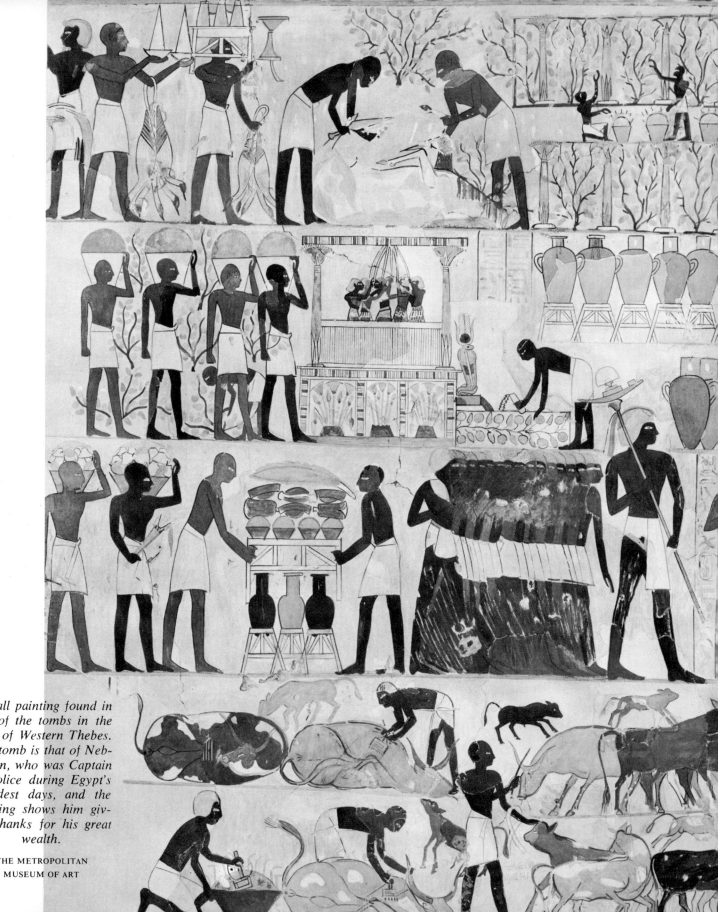

A wall painting found in one of the tombs in the cliffs of Western Thebes. The tomb is that of Neb-Amun, who was Captain of Police during Egypt's proudest days, and the painting shows him giving thanks for his great wealth.

THE METROPOLITAN
MUSEUM OF ART

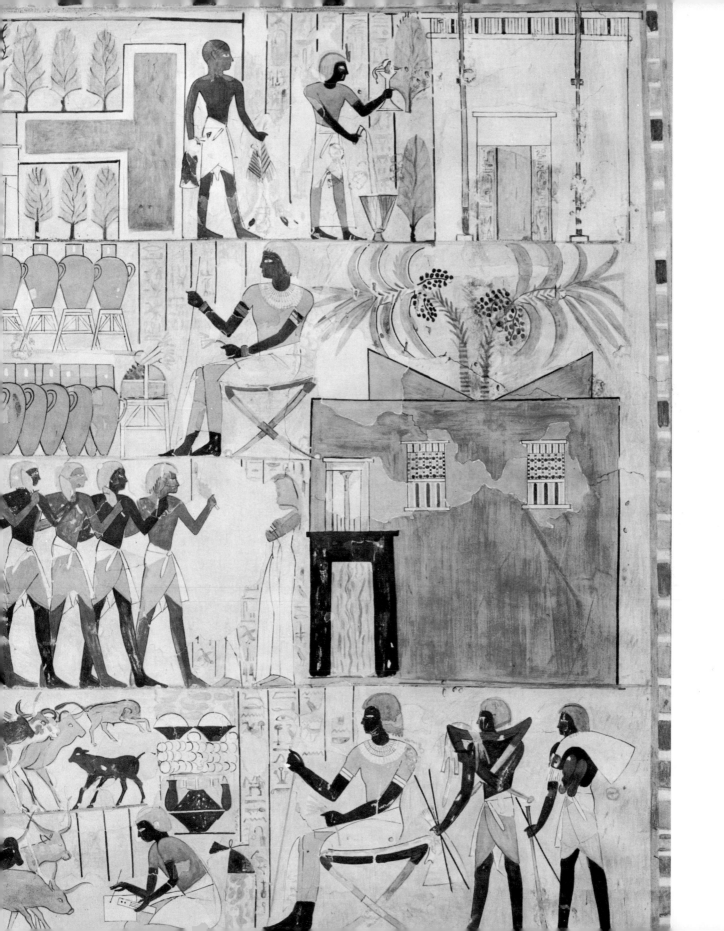

where the beloved god Osiris was supposed to have been buried, and where Egyptians came faithfully every year to watch scenes from his life re-enacted. Beyond Abydos, farther up the river, lay Dendereh. We know that Cleopatra went ashore here, for records show that the young queen offered sacrifices to the cow-goddess, Hathor, in the temple shrine which had been restored by order of her father, Auletes. And surely Caesar went ashore when they reached Koptos, some distance farther south, for this city would hold great interest for the Roman dictator.

Koptos was a gateway to the rich but almost unknown lands of the East. Sailing south on the Nile from Alexandria, merchants could disembark at Koptos and travel by camel caravan across the desert to the port of Berenice on the Red Sea. From there they could sail to the west coast of India.

Three hundred years earlier, after Alexander the Great had conquered Egypt, he had conquered part of India. Caesar had a deep admiration for Alexander and hoped to invade India himself some day at the head of a large army. Traveling through Egypt, which belonged to Cleopatra, would be far easier than fighting his way through enemy country. In Koptos he had an opportunity to gather information from men who had made the trip to India, and to question the leaders of camel caravans setting out across the desert.

Koptos was a bustling, noisy city. Thebes, about thirty miles farther south, was quiet. In the days of the greatest of the pharaohs, when Egypt was most powerful and prosperous, Thebes had been the capital. Now it lay partly in ruins, destroyed in a rebellion of the Egyptians against one of the Ptolemies and in other fighting. Yet some of the magnificent old temples were still standing, and the avenue of ram-sphinxes, which connected two of them, was intact. Colossal statues of long-dead

[42]

Ruins at Thebes of an ancient temple to the Egyptian goddess, Hathor.

pharaohs and slim obelisks stood stark against the blue Egyptian sky on the west bank of the river. Behind them were cliffs honeycombed with the tombs of noblemen. Beyond the cliffs lay the Valley of the Kings where a number of the pharaohs were buried. Since things of great value were buried with each pharaoh, in order that his spirit might live comfortably in the next world, many of the tombs had been plundered. But on their walls there still remained the pictures from which the world has learned much about the life of Egypt in its proudest days.

It was in Thebes, so one historian tells us, that a new bull awaited Cleopatra — a sacred bull which was the image of Montu, the God of War and the Lord of Thebes. With great ceremony the bull was escorted by priests to a sacred bark of Amon and put aboard. Then he traveled in style, accompanied by boats filled with priests, and by the ships in Cleopatra's fleet, to Hermonthis, which had once been an important city. In Hermonthis, Cleopatra herself presided over installing the sacred bull in his temple, made the usual sacrifices, and announced that some day she intended to build another temple there.

By this time Caesar's soldiers, all men of action, must have begun to tire of their leisurely journey. At any rate, when the fleet was at or near Aswan, more than seven hundred miles from Alexandria, orders were given to turn about and start north. The trip had been extremely pleasant for both Caesar and Cleopatra. She had seen her kingdom for the first time, and he, by asking questions constantly and observing keenly, now knew the extent and the wealth of the land over which his Egyptian wife ruled. Yet each must have been glad when the royal houseboat sailed into Great Harbor and they were back at last in Alexandria.

Caesar had been a long time away from Rome. As dictator, or head of the Roman Republic, he knew that there was much work awaiting him in Rome. Yet he did not leave Egypt at once, for he and Cleopatra were expecting a child. To the delight of both, their baby was a boy. They named him Caesar but he was called Caesarion, or little Caesar. He was also known to the Egyptians as Ptolemy XVI.

Caesar and Cleopatra had great dreams for the future when Caesar sailed away from Alexandria in the late summer of 47 B.C., soon after the birth of his son. Caesar was already master of Rome and all her provinces. Now he dreamed of subduing Parthia, a country lying between the deserts of Arabia and the Caspian Sea, and then of conquering India. When this had been accomplished, all the important countries in the world except Egypt would be ruled by him, and since he was married to the Queen of Egypt he would be the sole monarch of the known world.

Cleopatra hoped fervently that he could make his dreams come true, for then Egypt and Rome would be one great empire, which she and Caesar could rule jointly and which their son, Caesarion, would some day inherit.

Head and shoulders of a colossal statue of one of the pharaohs. Note the size in comparison with that of the man who stands at the right.

A view of Alexandria showing Cleopatra's Needle. This obelisk was first set up about 1500 B.C. at a city now called Heliopolis, by Thutmose III. Some Egyptian scholars think it was moved to Alexandria by Cleopatra after her journey with Caesar up the Nile. Others say it was moved there after her death by Octavian. It stands now in London, England, on the bank of the Thames River. Another like it is in Central Park in New York City.

IV. End of a Dream

Caesar had promised to send for Cleopatra as soon as he could do so, and she waited anxiously for news of him. At the same time she was supervising the care of her baby son and attending to affairs of state. Almost no records have been found which tell us what she did at this time, but the duties of any ruler of Egypt were many.

Dissatisfied people or those who wanted special favors sent petitions to the ruler from all parts of the country. Some appeared at the palace to present their petitions in person. It was the custom for the ruler or the Royal Secretary to read or listen to all such petitions and to decide what should be done about each one. It was the duty of the ruler to appoint officials to govern the various sections of Egypt, and to make sure that the priesthood was not gaining too much power over the people. The king or queen was also expected to make gifts to the temples of money or land, and to plan for the erection of new temples and monuments and for the repair and restoration of old ones.

In addition to all this, Cleopatra had to oversee the rebuilding of large parts of her beautiful capital which had been destroyed in the Alexandrian War. Damage done to the palace and to various public buildings was repaired. New buildings were set up to replace those which had been demolished. Canals which had been obstructed were opened. Streets were cleared of rubble, bridges were rebuilt, gardens and terraces were replanted, and the city was restored to order.

Such a tremendous project, which cost a great deal of money, took careful planning on the part of Cleopatra and her advisers. One can almost see the young queen on her throne listening patiently to some report or petition, and yet at the same

Slaves using shadufs to raise water from the Nile for irrigation purposes.

Caesar celebrates his triumph over Egypt. With two attendants, Cleopatra's sister, Arsinoe, walks ahead of his chariot in chains

time wondering when a ship would sail into the harbor bringing letters or messages from Caesar.

Although the Roman general was very busy, he managed to keep her informed of what he was doing, and the news she received from him was always good. He had put down a rebellion in Pontus, a Roman province in Asia Minor, and won a splendid victory there despite the fact that his forces were greatly outnumbered. He had returned to Rome in triumph and been received joyfully by the people. He had left Rome for Numidia in North Africa where friends of the dead Pompey had gathered an army to rebel against him. There again he had won a great victory after four months of hard fighting.

All of this brought joy to Cleopatra as she waited hopefully for a letter urging her to come to Rome. At last, in the summer of 46 B.C., that long-expected summons came. A Triumph, which was the highest honor Rome could pay to a victorious general, was to be celebrated in the city during August to honor Caesar. He had just been named dictator for the third time and he wanted Cleopatra and his son Caesarion to be there.

Happily the little queen began to prepare for her departure. Crowds gathered along the quays near the palace one bright summer day to watch her board her fast sailing ship with her courtiers, her servants, her baby son with his guards and nurses, and her eleven-year-old brother, King Ptolemy XV.

How long it took her to cross the Mediterranean we do not know. Caesar did not meet her in Ostia, which was the seaport for Rome, but in the city itself. Surrounded by the Roman Senators and other officials, he welcomed her, not as his wife, but as the Queen of Egypt. She and the baby, with the rest of the royal party, were escorted in state to the villa on the outskirts of the city which Caesar had prepared for her. It was a lovely place, surrounded by beautiful gardens, on the bank of the Tiber River; a place where Caesar could visit Cleopatra and Caesarion frequently.

Meanwhile, plans had been completed for Caesar's Triumph, which lasted four days. On the first day, from her seat of honor on the tribune, among high Roman officials, Cleopatra watched Caesar celebrate his victory six years earlier over the Gauls. Through streets filled with cheering crowds he led a long procession of Gallic prisoners, carts loaded with war trophies, and wagons filled with plunder. After dark he rode up the hill to the Capitol by torchlight, accompanied by forty elephants carrying the torch bearers. Vercingetorix, the leader of the defeated Gauls, was forced to walk in chains ahead of Caesar's chariot, and was killed by order of the dictator when the day's festivities ended.

On the following day Caesar celebrated his victory over the Egyptians in the Alexandrian War. Many things brought from Egypt, including wild animals which the Romans had never seen before, were displayed in the procession which followed him. This time the prisoner in chains who walked ahead of his chariot was Cleopatra's sister, the rebellious Princess Arsinoe. Although Cleopatra had never liked Arsinoe, she must have felt some pity for the young girl who shuffled past her now, with her head bowed in grief and shame.

Certainly the mobs of people pitied the young Egyptian princess, but they quickly forgot her as they enjoyed the lavish feast provided for them by Caesar. On the third day they watched a procession of prisoners and plunder from Pontus. On the fourth day the victory over the Roman army that had rallied around the friends of Pompey in Numidia was celebrated, and Caesar's Triumph came to an end.

Unfortunately, some of the displays in these processions caused the dictator to lose popularity among more thoughtful Romans. They felt that Caesar had shown poor taste in parading the sister of Egypt's queen through the streets. They disliked the fact that he had not only exhibited weapons taken from Romans in Numidia (who, after all, were his own countrymen) but also cruel caricatures of their dead Roman leaders. And there were some who resented the presence of Cleopatra in the city, especially the friends of Caesar's wife, Calpurnia. Although in Egypt it was legitimate for a man to have more than one wife at the same time, it certainly was not so in Rome.

Rumors of this displeasure on the part of prominent Romans must have reached Cleopatra in her villa on the bank of the Tiber and may have worried her. But Caesar was not worried. He delighted in visiting the villa where he spent many happy hours with Cleopatra and their little son. Even while he was busy governing Rome and her provinces, he was making plans for the Egyptian-Roman Empire which he intended to found and to pass on some day to Caesarion.

Cleopatra, during this period, posed frequently

for a famous Roman sculptor who was making a statue of her at Caesar's command. When the work was finished, the dictator had the statue placed in a magnificent temple which he dedicated to the Roman goddess, Venus, from whom he claimed to be descended. To celebrate this dedication there were more festivities with another lavish feast for the citizens, a show in the Roman Circus where gladiators fought each other and also wild beasts, theaters open to everyone in four parts of the city, and finally a sea fight on a man-made lake between Egyptian soldiers on Egyptian ships. It was a gala occasion for thousands of Romans, but the placing of Cleopatra's statue in the temple of Venus angered others who were already turning away from Caesar.

Talk about the dedication had hardly died away when trouble arose in the Roman province of Spain. Two of Pompey's sons and some of his friends, undaunted by the defeat in Numidia, were raising a large army there and preparing another revolt against Caesar. Appointing eight men to govern Rome in his absence, Caesar left with his own army to put down the rebellion. He was gone for several months, and during this time Cleopatra spent many anxious hours. She thought often about Caesar's friends and those who pretended to be his friends: Cassius, who tried to hide his hatred of Caesar when he came to call at the villa; Brutus, whom Caesar loved but who seemed too deeply influenced by Cassius; Cicero, who feared that Caesar was trying to gain too much power and who disliked Cleopatra; young Octavian, Caesar's favorite nephew, who was fighting beside his famous uncle in Spain; and Antony, who ten years earlier had marched into Alexandria and restored Cleopatra's father, Auletes, to his throne.

Of them all, Cleopatra placed the greatest trust in Mark Antony, who had risen in the army to be second in command under Caesar. Although the

Romans feasting, perhaps during the celebration of the dedication of the temple.

two men had quarreled recently, they had long been good friends, and when Caesar returned to Rome in the spring of 45 B.C., after another tremendous victory over the Pompeian forces, it was Antony who met him outside the city.

Again the great Caesar was widely acclaimed by the populace at another Triumph. This over, he turned his attention to governing Rome, reaching always, however, for more power. The people in Rome were sharply divided in their feeling about this. Unthinking Romans cheered wildly that winter when Caesar was appointed by the Senate as a dictator for life, and given a new title, Imperator. Others, who did not want the Republic of Rome to become a monarchy, feared that Caesar would some day gain enough power to have himself crowned as their king.

Cleopatra wished ardently for this. Despite the fact that she was uneasy about the increasing number of Caesar's enemies, she looked forward to the day when he would become a king and establish her as his queen, so that their dream of ruling an empire together might be fulfilled. It was a great disappointment, therefore, when Caesar told her some time in the late winter of 44 B.C. that he intended to leave Rome to lead an expedition against Parthia. He told her also that she must return to Egypt with Caesarion and remain there until he had conquered Parthia and made that country another Roman province.

Cleopatra began unhappily to make preparations for her long journey to Alexandria, wondering, no doubt, how many years would pass before she and Caesar could be together again. Meanwhile, Caesar showered her with presents and, when he was not making his own preparations for his march on Parthia, spent as much time as he could with her and little Caesarion.

Caesar was not well, his enemies in Rome were becoming more active, and rumors were being

The Senators flee in fear after the brutal assassination of Julius Caesar.

circulated in the city that there was a plot afoot to kill him. Cleopatra was filled with foreboding as she waited for March 17th, which was the day he planned to depart for the East. Her fears were justified on the 15th — the Ides of March — when someone brought her terrible news. Caesar, who had entered the Senate that day unafraid, in spite of evil omens and warnings from faithful friends that he was in danger, had been brutally stabbed to death by Cassius, Brutus, and a dozen other conspirators.

In a few brief minutes Cleopatra had lost the

Caesar's body was moved from the Senate to the Forum, and his friend, Mark Antony, who was now one of the chief magistrates in the Republic, took charge of everything. On the following day Antony opened and read Caesar's will. It was a surprise to everyone and a great shock to Cleopatra.

Caesar had left a small sum of money to every Roman citizen and had given all his great estates on the bank of the Tiber, including the villa in which Cleopatra was now living, to the Romans. The rest of his vast fortune was to be divided between three nephews, with the largest share going to Octavian, whom Caesar named as his adopted son and official heir.

Cleopatra, Queen of Egypt, had no need for money. But she was greatly distressed because Caesar had made no mention of Caesarion in the will and because, although he had intended to do so, he had never officially recognized the boy as his son. At her request, Mark Antony agreed to look after Caesarion's interests and announced in the Senate a few days later that Caesar had openly acknowledged Caesarion as his own lawful son.

For many days Rome was in a ferment over Caesar's death. News spread among the Romans that Octavian was coming to claim his inheritance, and the excitement grew. Thousands of people wanted to see Antony, who had sponsored little Caesarion, in power. Others favored Octavian, and the city seemed to be on the verge of civil war.

Cleopatra decided that she must leave for home with her son as quickly as possible. Toward the middle of April of 44 B.C. she and her royal party set sail for Alexandria. Her young brother, King Ptolemy XV, was not with her, for during her stay in Rome he seems to have disappeared, and there is no record to tell us how or why. Arsinoe, her sister, already had been sent to Syria by Caesar, exiled from Egypt for the rest of her life.

man she loved, her husband according to Egyptian law, the father of her three-year-old son, and the great leader with whom she had hoped one day to rule the world.

Rome was in turmoil. There was fighting in the streets, and terrified people fled to their homes.

V. A Wise and Glamorous Queen

When Cleopatra's ships sailed past the Pharos Lighthouse and into the Great Harbor of Alexandria, there were many loyal Alexandrians who were glad to welcome her back. Others spoke of her resentfully. She had been away from her own country for two years and what, they asked each other, had she accomplished? She had brought back no treaty of alliance with Rome. Caesar, on whom they had counted heavily for protection, was dead, and the old fear of a Roman invasion was awakened again in their minds.

As for the Egyptians throughout the land, most of them neither knew nor cared that their queen had returned. For two years there had been a "poor Nile." Great stretches of ground, which were usually flooded by the river and covered with life-giving silt, were dry and infertile. Farmers had been unable to plant sufficient crops, and now hunger stalked the land. Only in places where some far-sighted official had stored up great quantities of grain in better years did people have enough to eat. One of these wise officials was the Greek Viceroy of Thebes. Because of his prudence he had been able to help not only his own people, but thousands of others.

Reports of the famine which threatened her country reached Cleopatra soon after she was re-established in the palace. She took steps at once to buy food from other countries and to see that it was distributed freely where it was most needed. Then she turned her attention to complaints which were pouring into the palace against a new tax which had been laid on the people. On the advice of her ministers she decided that she could not abolish the tax, but when she heard that certain dishonest officials were forcing people to pay more than they should and keeping the excess for themselves, she had them dismissed from office and punished. Meanwhile she, like all other people living in Egypt, waited anxiously for the next flooding of the Nile, which usually began in June, and on which all Egypt was dependent. It must have been a "good Nile" that year, for we find no more records of famine.

These were difficult times for Cleopatra. She was still grieving over the death of Caesar, and still hoping that Mark Antony could prevent

Cleopatra makes an offering to the gods.

Cleopatra, seated in the audience hall of the palace, discusses a petition presented by one of her subjects.

Octavian from claiming his inheritance and would protect the interests of Caesarion. Impatiently she waited for news from Rome, but when it came it was often bewildering and seldom encouraging.

At first, Antony, whom the queen liked and trusted, had opposed Octavian and tried to make trouble for him in the Senate. Then the queen learned to her dismay that Antony and Octavian had patched up their differences. Both were ambitious, however, and each desired to get rid of the other in order to gain complete control of Rome and her provinces. So they quarreled again and, within a few months, were engaged in fighting a small war.

Cleopatra had no doubt that Antony would win. But soon she heard that, after a battle in which many lives were lost, Antony and Octavian had stopped fighting and had once more come to terms. With a man named Lepidus, they had formed a Triumvirate and were now ruling Rome jointly.

This reconciliation between Caesar's nephew and the man she had relied on to protect Caesarion caused the Queen of Egypt many hours of uneasiness. Yet her trust in Antony was not entirely shaken, and the next news which came to her was good. Leaving Lepidus in Rome, Antony and Octavian were leading a large army against Brutus and Cassius, who had fled to Greece soon after Caesar's murder and raised an army of their own.

The two armies met at Philippi near the western coast of Macedonia in October of 42 B.C. Octavian, who was a sickly young man, was taken ill before the battle, and Antony commanded the troops. As a general he had a reputation almost equal to that of Julius Caesar. He was extremely courageous, generous to his enemies as well as to his friends, and loved by his soldiers, who were as devoted to him as he was to them. They fought a hard battle at Philippi which lasted for several days. By the time it ended, Cassius had been killed

by one of his own men at his own command, Brutus had committed suicide, and Antony had won a great victory.

With the enemy forces destroyed or in flight, it was decided — probably by Antony — that Octavian should return to Italy. Antony himself, with a large army, set out for the East to impress the provinces there with the power of Rome and to collect tribute from their kings. His victory at Philippi had made him a great hero. He was a large, handsome, good-humored man whom most people were bound to admire, even when he sometimes drank too much or made vulgar remarks. And Cleopatra, in Alexandria, must have heard many reports of his slow, triumphal journey through Greece and into Asia Minor.

Late in the summer of 41 B.C., the queen received a message from Antony, brought to her palace by one of his officers, a Roman named Dellius. Dellius told the queen that Antony had set up headquarters at Tarsus, a city in Cilicia, across the Mediterranean Sea from Egypt, and wanted Cleopatra to come there so that they could talk together about matters which were of interest to them both.

Since Antony was rapidly becoming what Julius Caesar had once been — the most powerful man in the world — Cleopatra felt that she could not very well refuse this invitation. Nor did she wish to do so. She was anxious to find out from Antony why he had joined forces with Octavian. She wanted to know also if there was any chance that he might again be persuaded to champion the cause of little Caesarion. And she still had hope that, through some sort of alliance with him, her great ambition — that of establishing an Egyptian-Roman Empire which Caesarion would inherit some day — might yet be fulfilled.

Deciding that she must impress Antony with the wealth of her kingdom in order to make such an alliance seem profitable to him, Cleopatra spent some time in preparing for the voyage to Tarsus. Royal galleys were moored at the palace quay and loaded with all sorts of magnificent things. When all was ready the queen, with a large retinue of courtiers and slaves, set sail, leaving Caesarion, who was now six years old, in the care of his nurses and tutors.

The trip across the Mediterranean was made safely. Tarsus lay a few miles from the sea on the banks of the Cydnus River. Entering the river one morning, the royal Egyptian fleet slowly moved toward the city. There in a small harbor made by the widening of the river, Cleopatra's galleys dropped anchor. Immediately, news spread through the city that the Queen of Egypt had come. Men, women, and children rushed to the harbor to gape at her ships.

Antony, who was seated in the public market place settling disputes among various officials of Tarsus and listening to their complaints, saw the crowd around him melt away as his audience joined the people on the wharfs. On learning of Cleopatra's arrival, he dispatched an invitation to the queen at once to come ashore and dine with him. In reply, he received a message from Cleopatra inviting him to bring some of his officers and certain high-ranking men of Tarsus to dine with her aboard the royal galley that evening.

The sun was setting when Antony and his party arrived on the quay, which was still crowded with people. Strains of soft music and the fragrance of incense and perfumes drifted across the water to them, as Cleopatra's magnificent galley approached the shore, propelled by rowers using oars cased in silver. At the stern of the ship, under an elephant's head made of gleaming gold, two helmsmen worked the rudders, surrounded by lovely slave girls dressed as graces or sea nymphs. Cleopatra, looking more beautiful than ever, reclined on a gold-covered couch, clad in a shimmering gown like that worn by the goddess Venus, and

fanned with ostrich-plume fans by boys made up to represent Cupids.

This display of Egypt's riches and beauty was nothing, however, compared to what followed. That evening Antony and his friends dined in the ship's banquet hall. The floor had been strewn with flowers, the walls were hung with richly embroidered draperies, handsome couches were furnished for each guest, the dishes were all of dazzling gold inlaid with precious stones, and the food was rare and delicious. At the end of the evening, when Antony thanked the queen for the splendid entertainment, she gave him everything in the banqueting hall, including the golden dishes and draperies. The following evening, at another feast more lavish than the first, she presented each guest with the couch on which he had lain, the golden goblet and dishes which he had used, and either a litter with slaves to carry it, or a horse decked out in golden trappings.

After a third evening of feasting and revelry, Antony made a remark to the effect that such superb entertainment and such costly gifts must be a great drain on the royal treasury of Egypt. Whereupon Egypt's beautiful queen made a wager with him that at the following banquet she would spend 10,000,000 sesterces on food alone.

To the disappointment of guests who dined aboard the royal galley the next evening, nothing in the way of food appeared on the table which they had not seen before. But at the end of the banquet an attendant brought Cleopatra a small golden cup filled with vinegar. Taking off one of her magnificent pearl earrings, which was worth half of her wager, Cleopatra dropped it into the vinegar. The pearl dissolved quickly, and just as quickly Cleopatra drank it down. Almost speechless with astonishment, Antony and his friends prevented her from destroying the second pearl in the same way and agreed she had won her wager.

During the course of her visit, Cleopatra also

won Antony. Not only did she impress him with the riches of her kingdom, but he also fell in love with her wit, beauty, and charm. It did not matter to him that he had a wife in Italy and duties to the people of Rome. When Cleopatra returned home a short while later, Antony arranged his affairs in Tarsus as speedily as possible and followed her to Alexandria.

The fateful meeting between Cleopatra and Antony at Tarsus.

VI. For Egypt and Caesarion

Antony arrived in Alexandria early in the winter of 41 B.C., and at once Cleopatra set out to do everything in her power to entertain him. He was an honored guest at the palace, and the queen took great pride in showing him the beauties of her capital.

Together they visited the lovely open-air theater near the palace where pageants were given at the queen's command. They watched the games and chariot races in the vast Hippodrome on the sandy plains outside the city wall. They went to the beautiful temple of the Greek god, Pan. They climbed (or were carried in litters) up the hundred marble steps leading to the Shrine of Serapis to look at the colossal statue of Serapis, a god who was worshipped by Egyptians and Greeks alike. They went to the tomb of Alexander the Great where the founder of Alexandria lay in his golden coffin, and visited tombs of some of the Ptolemies who, like all Egyptian pharaohs, had prepared their Houses of Eternity while they still lived.

They talked with scholars in the museum and attended sessions in the law court. They watched boats arrive in Great Harbor loaded with corn which Egyptian farmers raised in such abundance that it was shipped abroad in big sailing vessels to feed the peoples of other lands.

They fished together on lovely Lake Mareotic or in the harbor or on the sea. They rode and hunted in the desert beyond the city. And sometimes when they wearied of sports and entertainment and feasting, they disguised themselves as servants and wandered through the streets of Alexandria at night in search of adventure and fun.

Meanwhile, Cleopatra had grown to love Antony more, perhaps, than he loved her. She had become his wife with the approval of the Egyptian courts and priesthood, and her greatest desire was to keep him with her. But Antony was badly needed elsewhere. In Italy, his Roman wife Fulvia was making serious trouble for him with Octavian.

Antony and Cleopatra as depicted on a coin.

Cleopatra and her son, Caesarion, as rulers of Egypt, pictured on the walls of a temple at Dendereh in the usual Egyptian style.

In Syria, some of the princes who resented Roman rule had combined forces with men from Parthia and were planning an attack on the Roman Governor of Syria. On receiving news of trouble in both places, Antony made preparations at once to leave Egypt.

Cleopatra was miserable at the thought of their coming separation and disturbed by his attitude toward her. Formerly he had shared her dream that together they would some day rule an empire

Papyrus plants from which the Egyptians made sheets of papyrus on which to write. In the background is part of one of the colossal statues.

made up of Rome and Egypt. Now he seemed to avoid making any plans for their joint future. He also seemed to treat their marriage very lightly, and when she told him that a child would be born to them during the coming fall, he showed little interest. One day in early March of 40 B.C. she watched his ship sail out of Great Harbor and disappear behind Pharos Lighthouse, not knowing where or when she would see him again.

Lonely and unhappy, Cleopatra now turned her attention to the affairs of her kingdom, which she had somewhat neglected during Antony's visit. Once more she was busy listening to petitions, acting as judge in certain types of legal cases, supervising the construction of new buildings in Alexandria, and arranging for contributions of money to both Greek and Egyptian temples. Although a great deal of money was needed for the expenses of her court, she did not lay excessive taxes on her subjects, as most Ptolemies had done. When a group of Alexandrians appeared before her, soon after Antony's departure, petitioning her for the right to farm outside the city walls without paying taxes, she passed a law allowing them to do it. She was a good ruler and her people loved her. She was a good mother, too. Carefully she supervised the training and education of little Caesarion, who was growing more like his father, Julius Caesar, every day.

She realized that, as a future ruler of Egypt, there were many things Caesarion must know. First he must know the history of his country, all about its rise and fall and how it had been captured by the Greeks. Next he must learn about the people who inhabited it; the patient Egyptians, the proud Greeks, the Arabs who had given up roaming the deserts and settled along the Nile, and the Jews of whom there were a great many in Alexandria alone.

Then he must learn to distinguish among the

important foreigners who came to his mother's court, to be able to tell from what lands they came, and to know whether or not they were friendly to Egypt. He must learn about the economy of Egypt, too: what part of the taxes was paid into the royal treasury and what part was spent on the people, the land, and the temples.

Sometimes Cleopatra arranged to have Caesarion sit near her while she held audiences with various officials who reported to her on the work of their departments. One official would tell the queen about canals which needed repairing and about the necessity of buying new water wheels with which the farmers raised water from the Nile to irrigate their fields. Another might outline for her the gain in the production of oil made from linseed and pumpkins; of papyrus, corn, wheat, barley, wine, and beer. A third might report on the output of the gold mines or stone quarries, while another, in charge of the Police Department, might explain to the queen the reasons for the decrease or increase of crime.

When these audiences were ended, Caesarion was probably required to report to his mother on what he had heard. If Cleopatra drove about Alexandria, or left the city for other parts of the kingdom, she frequently took Caesarion with her. The two spent many hours together. Yet, even in the company of her young son, Cleopatra's thoughts were often of Antony. Although he did not write to her, she kept track of his activities through her agents who were stationed in Syria and Italy.

Temples on the Philae Islands dedicated to the goddess Isis, from whom Cleopatra claimed to have been descended.

On leaving Alexandria, Antony had sailed directly to the Syrian city of Tyre, where he learned that the rebellious Syrian princes and their Parthian allies had already gained control of most of Syria and Phoenicia. Since Antony did not have enough troops available to put down this rebellion, he had sailed on to Greece. There, so Cleopatra was informed, he was trying to settle the quarrel which his wife Fulvia had begun with Octavian. Later Cleopatra learned that Fulvia had died.

This must have been joyful news for the Queen of Egypt. Now, at last Antony was free to marry her according to Roman law. Now, with her help, he could overthrow Octavian, whom they both hated, and gain control of Rome. Now, once more, there was a possibility that her dream of an Egyptian-Roman Empire which Caesarion would some day inherit might be fulfilled. Hopefully Cleopatra waited for Antony to return to Alexandria, or to ask her to come to him. But Antony did nothing of the kind.

Instead he came to terms again with Octavian. The two men arranged a treaty whereby Octavian should remain in Rome and rule the West, while Antony was to set up headquarters in Greece and rule the East. In order to make this treaty more binding and to establish their friendship more strongly, Antony also agreed to marry Octavian's sister, Octavia.

This was a bitter blow to Cleopatra. A report of Antony's wedding celebration reached her soon after twins — a boy and a girl — were born to her in the fall of 40 B.C. She named the boy Alexander Helios and the girl Cleopatra Selene. Then, determined to keep Egypt as strong as she could, for their sakes as well as for Caesarion, she went on bravely ruling her kingdom.

It was about this time that Cleopatra heard that strong tribes of greedy and restless Nabatean Arabs were preparing to invade Egypt by way of the northeastern border. At once she dispatched a large part of the Egyptian army to Pelusium to defend the border. Meanwhile, Parthians, encouraged by the successful rebellion of some of the Syrian princes against Antony, had pushed their way into Judea, and dethroned King Herod, who had been under Antony's protection. Hurrying to Egypt by way of Pelusium, Herod now asked Cleopatra for help.

Wisely, the Queen of Egypt decided to take no part in the affairs of Judea while her own country was in danger. Acting on the advice of Athenion, one of her generals, she commanded her army to take the offensive against the Nabatean Arabs. Marching into Arabia Petrea, the Egyptians succeeded in destroying or scattering the Arab forces, after some hard fighting, and returned in triumph to Alexandria. News of this victory spread slowly through Egypt, and Cleopatra became more popular with her people than ever before.

Antony, too, was popular with his subjects. He was living in Athens, Greece, with his Roman wife Octavia, enjoying life as he always did, and ruling the East in a kindly, easygoing fashion which made his people love him. Octavian, on the other hand, was hated by many of the people whom he ruled in Rome and the provinces of the West. He was at this time a cruel, ill-tempered man. At his command, so many persons in Italy were tortured or crucified that he was called the Executioner, and there were thousands in his realm who would quickly rise against him if they dared.

Of this Antony was well aware. He felt sure that the day was coming when he could overthrow Octavian. Since Lepidus, the third member of the Triumvirate, no longer had any real power, Antony would then become the sole ruler of the West as well as the East. In the meantime, he planned to invade and conquer Parthia. For this, however,

The battle with the Nabatean Arabs in Arabia Petrea.

he would need more money, men, and ships than he had at his command. His wife Octavia certainly could give him no such help, and she was such a meek, sweet woman that he was beginning to tire of her anyhow. So he sent her back to Rome, parting with her in a friendly way and not telling her that he intended some day to divorce her. Then he dispatched a gentleman named Fonteius Capito to Egypt to ask Cleopatra if she would meet him in Antioch on the Syrian coast.

Cleopatra did not hesitate to accept this invitation. Although she now had little faith in Antony, she still loved him, and she needed his friendship because of the protection he could give to her children and her country. She suspected that he might be planning to ask her for help of some kind, but she decided not to give it unless he agreed to three things. He must go through another marriage ceremony which would bind him to her more firmly. He must restore to Egypt some of the countries in the East which had once been part of the Egyptian Empire. And he must recognize that Caesarion was the rightful heir to the throne.

When Cleopatra joined Antony several weeks later, he agreed to grant her requests. Another marriage ceremony was performed, he promised that he would recognize Caesarion as his heir, and he gave to Cleopatra all the lands which had belonged to Egypt during the reigns of the most powerful pharaohs.

Cleopatra, having left the affairs of her country in good hands, now settled down happily in the beautiful city of Antioch with her husband. During the winter, Antony went on with his preparations for the expedition to Parthia, and in March he and his army were ready to leave. Cleopatra, who loved excitement and adventure, set out with them. Sometimes on horseback, sometimes in a litter, she accompanied Antony as far east as the

town of Zeugma on the Euphrates River. There they parted, and she was soon on her way to Egypt with her retinue of courtiers and attendants.

This time Cleopatra traveled by land so that she could see some of the countries which Antony had given her. When she reached Jericho in Judea, King Herod came to meet her. He had regained his throne with Antony's help, but he was furious because Antony had included parts of Judea in his gifts to Cleopatra. Concealing his anger, Herod asked the queen if she would rent these portions of

Judea to him. Cleopatra agreed, and they came to an agreement which seemed satisfactory to both.

Herod next invited the queen to travel through Judea by way of Jerusalem. Again she agreed, not knowing that the wily king was plotting to capture and kill her as she traveled along the wild, zigzag mountain road which led to that city. Only the remonstrances of Herod's councilors prevented him from carrying out this plan. They were horrified when he divulged his plot to them. Pointing out to him that Cleopatra held the highest rank of any woman in the world and that Antony would take swift revenge on anyone who harmed her, they persuaded him to give up his evil scheme. King Herod then politely escorted the Queen of Egypt to Pelusium and presented her with some balsam shrubs which were highly prized in Egypt as a source of medicine and perfume.

Cleopatra reached Alexandria safely and resumed her life in the palace. She hoped to hear soon from Antony and expected the news to be good.

Cleopatra bids Antony farewell at Zeugma.

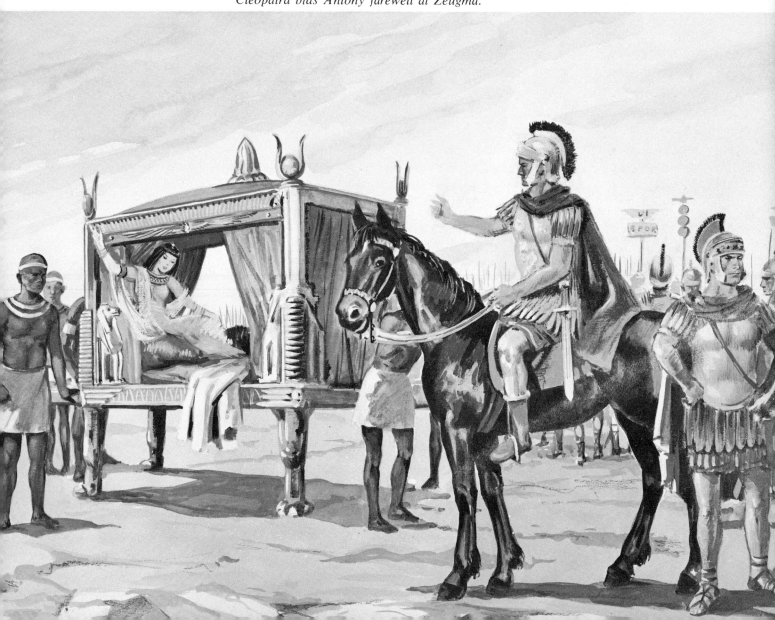

VII. Triumph and Trouble

The dispatches which were brought to Cleopatra for the next eight or nine months gave her grave cause for concern.

Antony's army consisted of nearly 100,000 men, including many Egyptians, and 13,000 foot and cavalry soldiers lent to him by the King of Armenia. Leaving part of this army to follow him with his train of heavy war engines, Antony succeeded in pushing deep into Media, a country which was allied to Parthia. There he stopped to lay siege to Phraata, the capital city of Media, and from that time on, disaster followed disaster.

All of Antony's war engines were captured, and the army accompanying them was badly defeated by Median and Parthian soldiers. The King of Armenia deserted and took his troops home. Parthian cavalry made swift attacks on the Romans and Egyptians who were besieging Phraata, harassing them constantly but refusing to do battle. Food supplies gave out, winter was rapidly approaching, and in October Antony was forced to order a retreat. Starving and in rags, he and the remnants of his army reached the coast of Syria after weeks of marching in bitter weather over mountains covered with snow.

After sending an urgent message to Cleopatra asking her for help, Antony set up winter headquarters in a place called White Hair and anxiously awaited her arrival. He had acted with great bravery on the long retreat, continually encouraging his men, caring for those who were wounded or ill, and sharing all their hardships. But when Cleopatra, with a fleet of ships loaded with food, clothing, and money, arrived at White Hair, she found that he had been drinking heavily and was in such a state of nervous depression that she took him home to Alexandria as soon as she could, to recuperate.

Many Egyptians had been killed during the ill-fated Parthian campaign, and the loss to Egypt in weapons and money was great. Yet so much wealth was produced every year by Egyptian farm-

A battering ram similar to those which were captured from Antony's army by the Medians and the Parthians.

Antony leads his men in the retreat from Media.

ers, miners, animal breeders, and manufacturers that Cleopatra was not forced to curtail her expenditures in any way.

Part of her great wealth was now used to refurbish her palace. The fine marble walls and pillars were decorated with agate and purple porphyry. Ceilings were fretted and inlaid with gold. Marble floors in some halls were replaced with floors of alabaster or onyx. Ebony doors were studded with emeralds. Couches and chairs were covered with rich fabrics, embroidered or threaded with gold, and were adorned with precious stones. Draperies made of luxurious materials imported from India or China were hung in various rooms, and tortoise shells from India were used to ornament some of the doors. Slave girls were bought for their beauty, slave boys for their good looks.

In these luxurious and peaceful surroundings, Antony regained his health and good spirits. He also became acquainted with his children, including the baby, Ptolemy, who had been born while he was besieging Phraata. Life in the palace was very pleasant and he had no desire as yet to leave Egypt. Surrounded by his own court, who had followed him to Alexandria, he governed his Roman provinces in the East from the Egyptian capital. This angered the Romans, who saw no reason why one of their rulers should live in a foreign land. They were angry, also, at the failure of Antony's costly expedition to Parthia and at his treatment of Octavia which had infuriated her brother Octavian.

The Romans placed much of the blame for Antony's actions on Cleopatra, and she became increasingly unpopular outside her own country. Her agents in Rome kept her informed of events there, and she felt sure that war between Octavian and Antony was inevitable. Indeed, she hoped for it, since she had little doubt that, with the wealth of Egypt behind him, Antony would be victorious.

Then, with Caesar's nephew out of the way, Caesar's son would inherit Caesar's fortune and political offices.

Quietly, Cleopatra encouraged Antony to rebuild his army and to replenish his treasury with money collected as taxes or tribute from his possessions in the East. When he wanted to go off on another expedition to Parthia, she kept him from it by refusing to eat and asserting that she would die if he left her. But when he decided, in the spring of 34 B.C., that the time had come to punish Artavasdes, the King of Armenia, for deserting him on the ill-fated Parthian expedition, she could not hold him back.

This time Antony was successful. He captured King Artavasdes and proclaimed Armenia a Roman province. Then, leaving a small army of Roman legionnaires in Armenia to keep order, he returned to Egypt with his prisoners and his loot. He was determined to celebrate his victory with a Triumph and to hold the Triumph in Alexandria rather than in Rome.

Great preparations were made in the Egyptian capital for this celebration. Early on the morning of the appointed day, in the fall of 34 B.C., Egyptians from near-by communities thronged into the city to witness the spectacle. With the Alexandrians, they crowded the streets and lined the wide avenues to watch a ceremony which had never before been held outside Rome.

The triumphal procession left the palace grounds early in the day to a fanfare of trumpets and drums. It was led by a body of legionnaires, each carrying a shield on which was emblazoned a large C. Behind the legionnaires, walked King Artavasdes and his wife and sons, weighed down by chains of gold. Antony followed these royal prisoners, riding in a magnificent chariot drawn by fine white horses, and followed in turn by a long line of captives, and wagons filled with loot.

Antony and Cleopatra argue about the expedition which he wants to make to Parthia.

Next in line of march came princes from Antony's vassal kingdoms in the East, each with a golden wreath or crown for the victorious Roman general. More legionnaires followed the princes, while troops of Egyptian soldiers, and soldiers from Antony's eastern provinces, brought up the rear.

To the cheering of thousands of Egyptians, the long procession made its way through the gaily decorated city streets and along the wide Boulevard of Serapis to the Shrine of Serapis. There Antony dismounted from his chariot and led his royal prisoners up the steps of the temple to present them to Cleopatra.

Dressed in the robes of the Egyptian goddess, Isis, the queen sat on a golden throne which had been placed before the temple entrance on a platform sheathed with silver. To the Egyptians she was indeed the goddess in human form, but she was not so to King Artavasdes. When he was ordered to prostrate himself before her and to address her as a goddess, he refused to obey, or to allow the members of his family to obey. Standing proudly erect, he spoke quietly to the queen, calling her by her own name. Such behavior on the part of the defeated king might well have caused either Antony or Cleopatra to order him

put to death at once. But both were so filled with admiration for his courage and dignity that his life and the lives of his family were spared.

The people jeered at these royal prisoners when they were led away by their guards, but quickly forgot them as the procession broke up and a huge banquet was laid out for all who wished to partake of it. Later, thousands of people flocked to the grounds of the big Gymnasium to watch another ceremony. This time they saw Cleopatra and Antony seated together, side by side on golden thrones. Near them, on smaller thrones of gold, were Caesarion, six-year-old Alexander Helios, looking very uncomfortable in an Armenian cloak and high tiara, his twin sister Cleopatra Selene, and the baby, two-year-old Ptolemy, who was dressed in a Macedonian costume and a diadem.

Standing before the crowds, Antony made a

Antony leads the triumphal procession through the streets of Alexandria.

long speech in which he announced that Cleopatra was not only the Queen of Egypt but of all the lands he had given her in Syria and the East, and that her son Caesarion was to rule with her jointly under the title, King of Kings. Next he told the cheering populace that he was giving his own son, Alexander Helios, the kingdoms of Armenia and Media, and Parthia as soon as it was conquered. To his daughter, Cleopatra Selene, he gave Libya and other parts of Africa, while little Ptolemy was presented with Phoenicia, and parts of Syria.

All of this delighted the Alexandrians and the other Egyptians who had come from outlying towns to watch the celebration. But that which pleased the Egyptians infuriated the Romans. Antony reported by letters to the Roman Senate on his victory in Armenia, his Triumph in Alexandria, and his distribution of Roman territories. When these letters were made public, many men declared hotly that Mark Antony had insulted his country by holding his Triumph outside of Rome. They asked angrily what right he had to give away provinces which belonged to Rome. They accused him of living like an eastern potentate instead of like a Roman ruler, and they announced that he did not know what he was doing because he was always drunk.

Most of the blame for Antony's actions, they placed on Cleopatra. Octavian made bitter speeches against her in the Senate, and slanderous stories about her were circulated through all of his provinces. There is no doubt that some of these stories were repeated to Cleopatra, but she probably paid no attention to them, for she had more important things to think about.

Antony *was* drinking too much. To the amusement of many Egyptians, he was also behaving very foolishly, driving through the streets of Alexandria on festival days dressed like the Greek god of wine, Bacchus. On other important occasions he insisted on walking beside Cleopatra's litter,

talking to the servants, instead of riding in state as he should. When he was sober, he worried about Octavian, who was constantly trying to turn all Romans against him and to start a quarrel which would lead to war.

At last Antony realized that such a war could not honorably be postponed much longer. He decided to take up winter quarters in the town of Ephesus, which was in Asia Minor on the coast of the Aegean Sea. Then he sent messengers to all the provinces and vassal kingdoms over which he had control, directing their governors or rulers to bring their armies to this meeting place.

Meanwhile, Cleopatra was also rallying the forces of Egypt. Within a few weeks two hundred Egyptian warships and many supply ships, loaded with corn, other foods, weapons, and munitions, were anchored in Great Harbor or in surrounding waters. Soldiers and sailors from towns and villages along the Nile poured into the city. Slaves

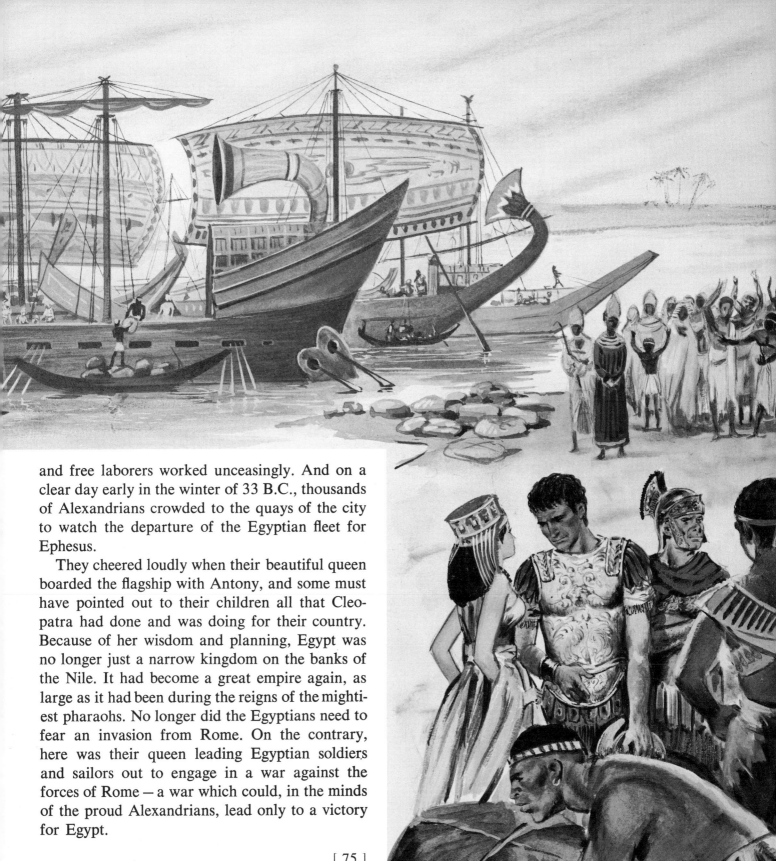

and free laborers worked unceasingly. And on a clear day early in the winter of 33 B.C., thousands of Alexandrians crowded to the quays of the city to watch the departure of the Egyptian fleet for Ephesus.

They cheered loudly when their beautiful queen boarded the flagship with Antony, and some must have pointed out to their children all that Cleopatra had done and was doing for their country. Because of her wisdom and planning, Egypt was no longer just a narrow kingdom on the banks of the Nile. It had become a great empire again, as large as it had been during the reigns of the mightiest pharaohs. No longer did the Egyptians need to fear an invasion from Rome. On the contrary, here was their queen leading Egyptian soldiers and sailors out to engage in a war against the forces of Rome — a war which could, in the minds of the proud Alexandrians, lead only to a victory for Egypt.

[75]

The proud Egyptians watch Antony and Cleopatra prepare to embark for Ephesus.

VIII. Terrible Days

Soon after the arrival of the Egyptian fleet in the harbor of Ephesus, Antony's own fleet began to assemble there. Warships and supply ships arrived daily from Syria and other eastern provinces, and the roads to Ephesus were clogged with marching men as thousands of soldiers poured into the great camp near the city.

Octavian, too, was gathering his army and navy together. He continued to make bitter speeches against Antony and Cleopatra in the Roman Senate and urged all Senators who sided with them to leave the city. In the spring, four hundred Roman Senators traveled to Ephesus to join Antony in fighting Octavian. They were surprised to find the Queen of Egypt at the headquarters with Antony and shocked to learn that he made no decisions regarding the army without consulting her. Telling him that many Romans who were still loyal to him would desert his cause if they discovered that he was dependent on a woman they had learned to hate, they begged him to send Cleopatra back to her own country.

To this Antony readily agreed, but Cleopatra, who had twice seen him come to terms with Octavian and who knew that the failure of this expedition would be disastrous for her and for Egypt, pluckily refused to go. Soon she learned that Octavian had formally declared war against her, announcing in the Roman Senate that Antony had lost his senses because of philters which she had given him, and was no longer fit to hold a public office of any kind. This only strengthened Cleopatra's decision not to leave her husband, and when Antony moved his army to Patrae, Greece, in the winter of 32-31 B.C., Cleopatra went with him.

Together they set up headquarters in Patrae and sent their fleets farther north to take shelter from the winter storms in the Gulf of Ambracia. Unfortunately, food supplies for the men of the

Octavian speaks bitterly against Cleopatra in the Roman Senate.

Cleopatra refuses to leave Antony and return to Egypt.

[77]

fleets ran low, and before the winter ended more than one-third of Antony's sailors and oarsmen were dead of various illnesses. News of this disaster and a report that Octavian was marching with a huge army down the coast of Macedonia toward the gulf reached Cleopatra and Antony in the early spring. As quickly as possible, they moved their army to Actium, a cape on the southern side of the gulf, where they established their camp. Octavian set up his camp on the northern side of the gulf and stationed his ships near its entrance in such a position as to blockade the fleets of Antony and Cleopatra.

After several months of inactivity, except for a few minor skirmishes which Octavian's soldiers won, Cleopatra persuaded Antony to try to break the blockade, despite the protests of his generals, who urged him to fight the enemy on land. Having decided on a sea battle, Antony ordered that every ship which was not needed in the fray, including all but sixty of the Egyptian ships, should be burned so that they might not fall into the hands of the enemy. What further plans he made for the battle, no one knows. Nor does anyone know why he and Cleopatra behaved as they did on the day of the great fight. This is what happened.

On the morning of September 3, Antony's ships, carrying 20,000 legionnaires and 2,000 archers, sailed forth to meet Octavian's fleet, which had been moved a short distance out to sea. Cleopatra followed with the Egyptian fleet.

Octavian's ships were small and swift. Antony's were bulky and well protected with great blocks of timber which were bolted to their sides, but which made speedy maneuvers impossible. Like mosquitoes, Octavian's vessels closed in on them. Fighting at close quarters with spears, javelins, and flame-throwers, Octavian's men captured, burned, or sank a number of Antony's ships. The

The battle at Actium with some of Antony's ships aflame.

men on Antony's other ships, however, continued to fight on bravely, catapulting missiles down on the enemy from the high wooden towers on their decks. Cleopatra's fleet was also engaged in the battle, which raged for several hours. Then suddenly, perhaps because she was overcome by the horrible sights and sounds of war, or perhaps because she feared that Octavian's ships were winning and wanted to save her fleet, Cleopatra signaled her captains to hoist sail and head south toward Egypt. Seeing the Egyptian ships in flight, Antony, to the amazement of his officers, made ready to flee, too. Deserting the battle, which had not yet been definitely decided one way or the other, he boarded his fastest galley and ordered the captain to overtake Cleopatra's flagship.

At dusk, Cleopatra saw the galley approaching and recognized Antony on the deck. She signaled to have him taken aboard her flagship and then went directly to her cabin, sick with the realization that, without a leader, the battle would surely be lost. Antony, who was sunk in despair and knew that his reputation was now ruined for

life, sat for three days in the prow of the ship, staring gloomily out to sea. When the Egyptian fleet reached the desolate port of Paretonium, some distance west of Alexandria, he decided to remain there, leaving Cleopatra to go on without him.

The queen was anxious to reach Alexandria before any report of the battle of Actium could be spread through the city. With pennants flying in the wind and musicians aboard her flagship playing gay music, she sailed into Great Harbor as though she were returning victorious from the war. By the time the Alexandrians learned what had really happened, she was in firm control of her kingdom once more, and anyone who protested too vigorously against the loss of Egyptian lives, money, or prestige was promptly imprisoned or put to death.

Expecting that Octavian would soon push south to carry on his war against her, Cleopatra knew that she must make every possible effort to save Egypt and her throne. King Artavasdes of Armenia had been in prison since the day of Antony's Triumph. For fear that he might escape and join Octavian, Cleopatra had him beheaded. She also ordered that all ships in her navy should be dragged over the sand to the Gulf of Suez where Octavian could not get his hands on them, and that other ships should be built at Suez. However, the Nabatean Arabs soon put a stop to this. Remembering their defeat by Egyptian soldiers several years earlier, they raided the docks, killed the boat builders, drove away the troops sent to protect them, and burned the ships which had been brought over the desert.

Cleopatra, who had already taxed her people heavily for this venture, was forced to abandon it, but she did not lose heart. Even the news that Antony's entire army in Actium had surrendered to Octavian did not discourage her from continuing to make brave plans for the future.

Antony broods over the disgrace which he has brought upon himself by fleeing from the battle.

Caesarion was soon to be seventeen years old, and she decided to mark his birthday with a great celebration and a proclamation to the Egyptian people that their King of Kings, who was also Caesar's son and rightful heir, had come of age and they now had a grown man to rule them. This she insisted on doing, despite the fact that Antony objected to it, for fear that it might irritate Octavian.

Antony had left Paretonium after several weeks and, having decided that he hated all mankind, was living in a little house which Cleopatra had built at his request on the end of a long pier jutting out into Great Harbor. Now he decided to move back into the palace where he could enjoy the birthday celebration even though he did not approve of it. It was a gala affair which lasted for several days, with plenty of feasting and fun for all, and the Alexandrians soon forgot the threat of war which hung over their country.

But Cleopatra could not forget it. She knew that Octavian was now in Asia Minor, preparing to invade Egypt, and that if he succeeded in doing it he would show her little mercy. Preferring to die rather than be captured by him, she began to investigate ways of committing suicide, watching the effects of fatal drugs on condemned prisoners and forcing some of the prisoners to allow themselves to be bitten by poisonous snakes.

In May she learned that Octavian had reached Syria, and she decided that, for his own safety, Caesarion must leave Egypt at once. She arranged for him to travel in state up the Nile to Koptos and then across the desert to Berenice on the Red Sea where he was to await the ships she planned to send to carry him and his party to India. There she hoped he would make alliances with the rulers of the Far East which would be helpful to him in the future. Their parting must have been a very difficult one, for Cleopatra well knew that she might never see her son again.

[81]

Caesarion had been gone only a short time when Cleopatra and Antony both sent messages to Octavian. Cleopatra promised to surrender to him peacefully if he would allow Caesarion to rule Egypt, unmolested. Antony, who was again drinking heavily, merely asked if he might be permitted to live as a private citizen either in Alexandria or Athens. Octavian made no reply to Antony, but sent word secretly to Cleopatra that he would listen to her proposal if she would have her husband killed. Although Antony had treated her badly and she could not rely on him, Cleopatra still cared for him, and Octavian's proposition fell on deaf ears.

Day by day, Octavian and his army were advancing farther south. Toward the middle of July, word was brought to the palace that the fortress of Pelusium had surrendered to him. Terrified Alexandrians huddled in their homes or went about their daily work in fear of what the next hour might bring.

Cleopatra, following the age-old custom of all

Cleopatra sadly bids farewell to Caesarion.

rulers of Egypt, had already built her tomb and a temple in which sacrifices could be made to her spirit after she died. These beautiful buildings of marble, granite, and rare woods had been erected very near the Temple of Isis, which was close to the palace. Now the queen had her priceless jewels and her most precious treasures of gold, silver, ebony, ivory, silks, and foreign spices moved to an upper room of her mausoleum. There they were placed on a pile of faggots so that they could be destroyed by fire before Octavian could lay hands on them. Since Cleopatra had decided to flee to the tomb if her enemy should capture Alexandria, she also had a chamber on the second floor of the tomb prepared for her.

The walled city was well fortified. Four Roman legions, left behind when Cleopatra and Antony had sailed to Ephesus, were there to defend it, and so was a large body of Egyptian soldiers. All of Antony's ships which had escaped from Actium lay in Great Harbor.

In late July, Octavian and his vast army encamped just east of the city. Now for a brief period Antony showed the courage for which he had once been famous. At the head of his four Roman legions, he rode out of the city and boldly attacked Octavian's cavalry, which was approaching the eastern wall. In the skirmish which followed, many of Octavian's men were killed. The others retreated in great confusion. Overjoyed with this success, Antony hurriedly returned to the palace and, still wearing his armor, which was dirty and bloodstained, caught Cleopatra up in his arms and kissed her, while the men who were with him looked on. Then he drew the queen's attention to one of his officers, who had fought with exceptional bravery. To reward this officer, Cleopatra gave him a helmet and breastplate of gold. That night, wearing his new golden armor, the officer deserted to the enemy.

Other men had deserted Antony before and

Antony boldly attacks Octavian's cavalry outside the walls of Alexandria.

Antony dies in Cleopatra's arms.

after the battle at Actium; some because they were alarmed by his erratic behavior, some because Octavian had bribed them, some for other reasons. Soon Antony was to face the greatest desertion of all.

Early on the morning of August 1, two days after routing Octavian's cavalry, Antony led his troops again through the eastern gates of the city and drew them up in battle formation on a hill not far from the sea. He had already given orders that his war galleys should attack Octavian's fleet that morning, and he watched them hopefully as they sailed out of Great Harbor to meet the enemy. Then, to his horror, he saw his Egyptian seamen salute Octavian's seamen with their oars. The salute was returned at once. The ships in Antony's fleet faced about, and both fleets advanced together on Great Harbor. At that same time, all of Antony's cavalry suddenly galloped off to join Octavian's forces. Now there was only the infantry left and it was no match for the enemy. Losing all hope, Antony, accompanied by a few of his officers, rushed back to Alexandria, riding at breakneck speed through streets filled with startled people, straight to the palace.

Cleopatra, who was anxiously waiting there for news of the battle, heard him enter, shouting for her, raging at her, cursing her, and crying out that she had betrayed him to Octavian. Terrified that he would kill her while he was in this unreasonable fury, she fled with two of her waiting-women down the palace halls, across the courtyard, and into her tomb. The guards and servants, frightened by the uproar and the news of the mass desertion, which was rapidly spreading through the city, had run away from their posts. With no one to help them, the panic-stricken queen and her two women, Charmion and Iras, managed to bolt and bar the heavy doors of the tomb before they ran up the stairs to the second floor. On reaching her chamber, Cleopatra must have announced that she was going to commit suicide, for Iras and Charmion, seeing some of Antony's men beneath an open casement window, called down to them that the queen was about to kill herself.

In the excitement of the moment, the words were misunderstood and someone ran to Antony to tell him that the queen had taken her own life. Shocked by this statement, Antony forgot his threats and false accusations. Crying out to those around him that there was no reason for him to live when Fate had taken away the only thing for which he wanted to live, he rushed to his bedroom, tore off his armor, and stabbed himself with his sword, falling unconscious across his bed.

An Egyptian servant ran to Cleopatra to tell her that Antony had wounded himself badly but was still alive. Immediately, the queen sent a message to her husband that she, too, still lived and would like to have him brought to her. Antony, who had regained consciousness and was in great pain, ordered slaves to take him to the queen.

Laying him on a makeshift stretcher, the slaves carried him to Cleopatra's mausoleum. The queen and her two women either could not open the door to the tomb or were afraid to do so, and Cleopatra directed that Antony be brought in through the window of her room on the upper floor. How this was done, no one seems quite sure. One biographer says that Cleopatra let down ropes and cords to which Antony was fastened and then, with the help of Iras and Charmion, pulled him up while the people standing below shouted encouragement. Another thinks that some of those people must have brought ladders and lifted Antony up at least part way. At any rate, he was dragged through the window, bleeding profusely and suffering intensely. A short time later, just as the first of Octavian's officers arrived in the palace courtyard, Antony died in Cleopatra's arms.

IX. Death Cheats Octavian

Antony's blood-stained sword and the report of his suicide already had been carried by one of the palace servants to Octavian. Fearing that Cleopatra, too, would kill herself, thus making it impossible for him to exhibit her in his Triumph in Rome, Octavian immediately commanded an officer named Proculieus to hasten to the queen and place her under guard as quickly as possible.

Antony had been dead only a very few minutes when Proculieus arrived at the mausoleum and began pounding on the door, announcing in a loud voice that he had an important message for Cleopatra from Octavian. Weeping bitterly for her husband and afraid that Proculieus had come to take her prisoner, Cleopatra went down the stairs. She called through the closed door, telling Proculieus that she would not admit him until she had a promise from Octavian that he would give Egypt to Caesarion. Proculieus assured her that she could trust Octavian to treat her honorably. Then, being unable to get into the tomb, he left, only to return a little later with a man named Gallus and two other officers.

This time it was Gallus who knocked and called for Cleopatra. With Charmion and Iras, the unhappy little queen went down again to the door, which she either could not or would not open.

Standing on the outside, Gallus engaged her in a conversation while Proculieus and his two companions climbed through the window of her upper chamber, by means of a ladder, and ran swiftly down the stairs. One of the waiting-women saw them coming and cried out to her mistress. Instantly, Cleopatra snatched a dagger from the sheath which hung at her waist and tried to plunge it into her heart. But Proculieus was too quick for her. Grabbing her arm, he shook the dagger from her hand and held her while his companions searched her to see that she had no other weapons and no poison concealed in her clothes. Then,

Proculieus pounds on the door of Cleopatra's tomb, shouting that he has a message from Octavian.

[87]

after ordering the tomb door unbarred and stationing sentinels outside, Proculieus allowed Cleopatra and her women to go upstairs, placed a guard over them, and left to report to Octavian.

He, meanwhile, had been preparing for his triumphal entry into Alexandria. Shortly before the sun set, he marched through the gates of the Egyptian capital to the grounds of the great Gymnasium, where he mounted a platform which had been erected for the occasion. At once all the people who had dared to leave their homes fell prostrate before him, just as Egyptians had always fallen before their pharaohs. Commanding them to stand, Octavian told them that he placed no blame on them for the war which had been waged against him and that, because of his friendship with one of their Alexandrian philosophers, he would spare as many lives as possible. Later, in order to impress the Egyptians still further with his kindness, he permitted Cleopatra to give Antony a royal burial in a tomb not far from her own.

When the funeral rites for her husband were over, Cleopatra returned to her mausoleum, so exhausted by grief and anxiety that she became very ill and was delirious for several days. During this time, and even after she regained her senses, she refused all food and begged her doctor again and again to let her die. This alarmed Octavian, who sent word to her that if she did not make an effort to recover her health, he would kill her children whom he was keeping under guard at the palace. Faced with this terrible threat, Cleopatra began to eat again and slowly grew stronger.

On August 28th, Octavian paid her a visit, unannounced. He found her lying on her bed and talked with her for some time, during which she pleaded with him to let Caesarion rule Egypt and to be merciful to her other children. Octavian assured her that she need expect only the kindest treatment from him for herself and her family.

[88]

Octavian reassures the terrified Alexandrians.

When he left, he believed he had convinced the queen that he meant what he said and that, as a result, she seemed eager to live. But, although Cleopatra had fooled Octavian, she had not been deceived in any way by his words or his manner. She felt sure now that he would never give up the throne of Egypt to Caesarion and that he intended to take her to Rome to exhibit her in chains before crowds of jeering people on the day of his Triumph.

A Roman officer named Dolabella, who had sometimes guarded the queen and who admired her greatly, had promised Cleopatra that he would keep her informed of any move Octavian might make toward sending her out of the country. On the very afternoon of Octavian's visit, Dolabella managed to get a secret message to the queen. In it he reported that Octavian, having seen for himself that Cleopatra was well enough to travel, planned to ship her and her children to Rome within three days. Dolabella may also have reported at this time that officers had been dispatched earlier in the month to overtake Caesarion before he set sail for India, and to bring him back to Alexandria where he would be murdered.

Overcome with despair on receiving his message and realizing that there was nothing more she could do for her children or for Egypt, Cleopatra decided to kill herself. First, however, she wanted to visit Antony's tomb. Octavian gladly gave her permission, and the following morning she was carried in her litter to her husband's final resting place. After a brief and tearful visit, she placed flowers on his gravestone and returned sorrowfully to her mausoleum. There she ordered Iras and Charmion to help her bathe and arrange her hair. Then she ate her last meal, wrote a letter which she sent by a messenger to Octavian, and told all of her servants to leave her, except Iras and Charmion, who closed the door of her room.

It did not take long for Cleopatra's letter to reach Octavian. On reading that she begged to be buried in the same tomb with Antony, he guessed at once what had happened and sent officers to the tomb in great haste to find out if it

The death of Cleopatra,

were true. Pushing past the sentries, who had no idea that anything was wrong, they ran up the stairs and burst open the door of Cleopatra's chamber.

There, on her golden couch, dressed in her robes of state and wearing her finest jewels, the Queen of Egypt lay dead. Iras was lying on the floor at her feet, just drawing her last breath, and Charmion stood beside the queen, feebly trying to straighten her crown. A moment later, she, too, fell to the floor and died.

How Cleopatra and her waiting-women had killed themselves, no one will ever know. The most widely accepted story is that, before her meal, a peasant brought the queen a basket of ripe figs in which a deadly asp was concealed and that Cleopatra allowed the snake to bite her. Another story is that Cleopatra already had such an asp hidden in a pitcher or vase in her room and teased it until it plunged its fangs into her arm. But if the queen was killed by the bite of an asp, what caused the deaths of her faithful waiting-women, and why was no snake ever found in her tomb? There is a third story that Cleopatra had secreted a fatal poison in a hollow needle or comb and that she shared it with Iras and Charmion.

Whether it was snakebite or poison, the end was the same. Egypt's queen had died bravely. Even Octavian, who had been cheated out of the pleasure of triumphantly displaying her in chains, admired her pride and her courage. He ordered that she be buried in Antony's tomb with all the splendor and magnificence due her rank.

Soon after the burial of his royal mother, Caesarion arrived in Alexandria. He had come willingly, for he had been told that Octavian wished him to return so that he might take his rightful place on the throne of Egypt. But as soon as he reached the capital he was seized by Octavian's agents and killed. Cleopatra's three younger children were sent to Rome under guard to be exhibited on the day of Octavian's Triumph. All of her beautiful treasures were confiscated and much of her gold and silver was melted down to be converted into money with which Octavian

Egypt's last queen.

could pay his troops. When the conqueror of Egypt returned to Rome the following spring, he was probably the richest as well as the most powerful man in the world.

In 27 B.C., Octavian was given the name Augustus to which he added the name Caesar. Later he became the first Emperor of Rome. Although Augustus Caesar ruled Egypt from Rome, he never declared the country a Roman province. Like the Ptolemy kings and queens, he considered the land along the Nile as his personal domain.

The Egyptians did not resent this. They thought of Augustus Caesar as the founder of a new dynasty and carved his name in hieroglyphics on their temple walls, giving him such pharaonic titles as "King of Upper and Lower Egypt," "Son of the Sun," and "Beloved of Ptah and Isis." They did not consider themselves as vassals of a foreign ruler, but rather as subjects of their own pharaoh, who was also ruling Rome.

And so, although it was not all that she had hoped for, Cleopatra's dream of an Egyptian-Roman Empire had in a strange, unhappy way come true.

Octavian, conqueror of Egypt, returns in triumph to Rome.